BELONG

MW01063730

# Praise for *Belong*

"If you want to belong, read this book."
—*Deepak Chopra*, MD

"Radha wrote a book that's fun to read, easy to digest, and embodies deep wisdom. I couldn't wait to finish reading my copy so I could give it to one of my friends to read the same day."
—*Tony Hsieh*, CEO of Zappos and author of Delivering Happiness

"This year America's happiness dropped as healthcare costs continue to soar. Radha has a solution for both. Her engaging, high-energy approach to connecting people and helping them provide purpose and find their community is an antidote more powerful than any pharmaceutical. *Belong* combines engaging storytelling, solid research, and an easy prescription for finding your tribe and harnessing its incredible healing powers. Read it and live longer, better!"
—*Dan Buettner,* National Geographic *fellow and* New York Times–*bestselling author of the* Blue Zones *books*

"Few people know how to live life with such authentic expression as Radha does. In this book she shows us, in a clear and fun way, how and why this way of life can lead us all to the very thing we as humans desire the most: to belong."
—*Alexander Ljung, Founder and Chairman, SoundCloud*

"Radha Agrawal is at the center of building one of the most important movements in America: the creation of deep community among a population of increasingly disconnected citizens. *Belong* takes the powerful lessons she's learned through her remarkable entrepreneurial journey and creates an essential guidebook for anyone who wants to create or be part of a thriving community among any group or around any cause."
—*Ben Rattray, Founder and CEO, Change.org*

"Radha was born to write this book. She has spent the last decade maniacally focused on figuring out the blueprint for community building, and this book cracks the code. Her illustrations make the book approachable and fun to read. I am so unbelievably proud of her achievement. It will help everyone find their tribe."

—**Miki Agrawal,** *Founder, Tushy, THINX, Wild,*
*and author of* Disrupt-her *and* Do Cool Sh*t

"When I was orbiting the earth every ninety minutes, I felt an incredible connection with the planet and all the earthlings living and working below. Reading *Belong* reminded me of that feeling of connectedness. I am certain this book will help readers reestablish meaning and purpose, together."

—**Leland Melvin,** *astronaut, S.T.E.A.M. Explorer, and author of* Chasing Space

Find Your People, Create Community &
Live a More Connected Life

# BELONG

## RADHA AGRAWAL

CEO & Co-founder Daybreaker
& Co-founder THINX

WORKMAN PUBLISHING · NEW YORK

Copyright © 2018 by Radha Agrawal

Illustrations copyright © by Radha Agrawal
Illustrated by Ryan LeMere and Radha Agrawal
Cover art by Tomas Garcia

All rights reserved. No portion of this book may be reproduced—
mechanically, electronically, or by any other means, including
photocopying—without written permission of the publisher.
Published simultaneously in Canada by Thomas Allen & Son Limited.

Library of Congress Cataloging-in-Publication Data is available.

ISBN 978-1-5235-0205-9

Design by Ryan LeMere, Janet Vicario, and Lisa Hollander

Workman books are available at special discounts when purchased in
bulk for premiums and sales promotions as well as for fund-raising or
educational use. Special editions or book excerpts can also be created
to specification. For details, contact the Special Sales Director at the
address below, or send an email to specialmarkets@workman.com.

Workman Publishing Co., Inc.
225 Varick Street
New York, NY 10014-4381

workman.com

WORKMAN is a registered trademark of Workman Publishing Co., Inc.

Printed in China
First printing July 2018

10 9 8 7 6 5 4 3

This book is dedicated to the
courageous and generous souls—
old and young—
who wake up every day to create and
serve their communities.
Thank you for enjoying the process,
not only the destination.
And to my future children,
I promise to create a world with you
in which you feel a deep sense
of belonging.

# You Have to Go In to Go Out

# Foreword

think I should start out by declaring my bias up front: I absolutely love this book! Radha Agrawal has written a book that is a reflection of who she is as a person—authentic, wise, adventuresome, and loving. *Belong* takes us on a journey to discover who we are, what we like and don't like, our purpose in life, and what gives us joy and happiness. It is our guidebook for exploration, and it shows us how to genuinely connect with others and create communities that we will nurture and which, in turn, will nurture us.

All of us were born into and grew up in various communities—our families, neighborhoods, schools, clubs, friends, religious groups, cities, our larger nation, and indeed the entire human race and perhaps even all sentient beings. We truly are tribal animals, and we can only fully flourish within communities where we truly belong. Despite our need and desire for authentic community, many of us no longer experience it in our lives. Many Americans are no longer close to their biological families, and the neighborhoods and communities that we grew up in may no longer be relevant to our lives. We all too frequently go forward on our life journey with little conscious understanding about the importance that belonging to various communities has for our health and happiness. *Belong* brilliantly shows us how to know ourselves better and find, create, and connect with the people and communities with whom we will find the greatest fulfillment. *Belong* is an incredibly empowering book because it puts the responsibility for finding and creating the communities that will fulfill us squarely on our own shoulders, while simultaneously teaching us the skills we need to do exactly that.

One of things I like best about *Belong* is that Radha shares her own life journey with us, and she does so with genuine warmth. Far from boasting about her many accomplishments, Radha tells us about the mistakes she has made and the lessons she has learned, turning us into the beneficiaries of her hard-earned wisdom. Often I felt her saying, "This is who I am. This is what I love and care about. This is what I want to do. This universe is beautiful and amazing! I want to share it with you. Let's create a fun and nurturing community together. Let's create a better world together."

*Belong* is overflowing with great ideas, wonderful stories, memorable quotes, and a depth of wisdom. I could quote dozens of lines I loved, but I'll limit myself to two of my favorite ideas, beautifully expressed here: "Energy is a great equalizer in life. It doesn't matter what you do for a living or how much money you have—the energy you put out is the energy you get back. Negative energy breeds negative community. Positive energy breeds positive community. It's that simple." And I also loved this: "As with everything in life, nothing stays the same. All communities and relationships evolve and change. When you sense it happening, rather than thinking, 'This isn't what it used to be,' consider this: It's never supposed to be what 'it used to be'! Everything evolves, including communities and relationships, and it's a beautiful thing! Let's learn to embrace that!"

*Belong* is an extraordinary book by an extraordinary person. It *can* be read quickly, but it should be read slowly, and, above all, it should be practiced. It is a book that will change your life for the better if you allow it to. I believe it has already done that for me; it has inspired me to lead my life adventure with more intentionality, more courage, and more love. I hope it does the same for you.

—JOHN MACKEY
CO-FOUNDER & CEO WHOLE FOODS MARKET

"We shall not cease from exploration. And the end of all our exploring will be to arrive where we started and know the place for the first time."—*T. S. Eliot*

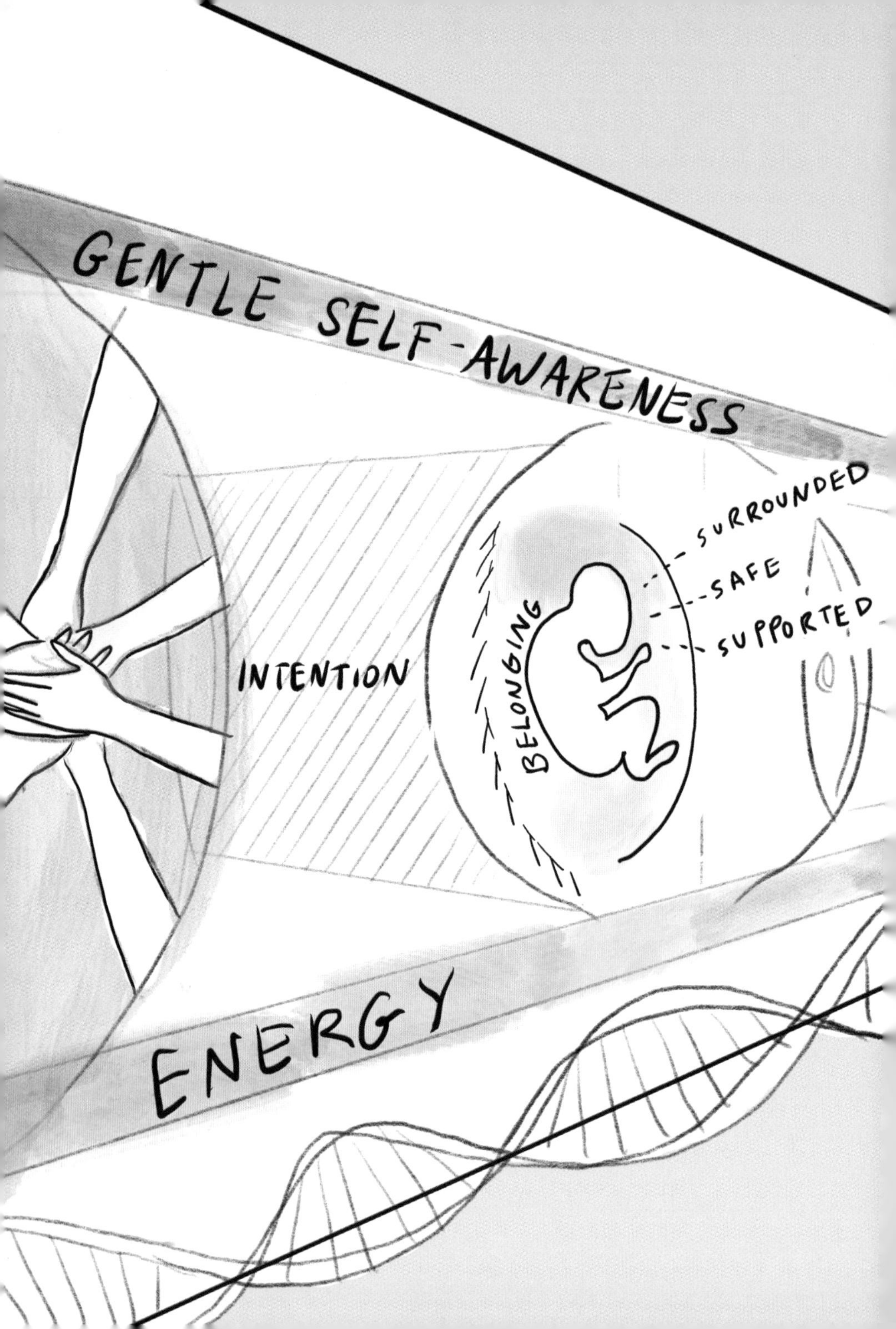

GENTLE SELF-AWARENESS

INTENTION

BELONGING

SURROUNDED

SAFE

SUPPORTED

ENERGY

PART I

# GOING IN

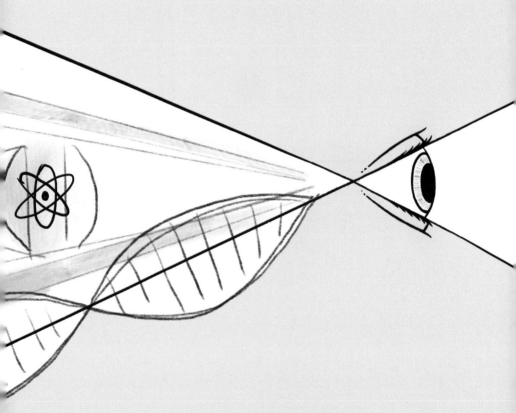

We are born in community—fully connected to another human. Without connection, we cannot survive. It's in our DNA to belong.

I didn't always understand
the importance of community.
My epiphany came at age thirty.

# CHAPTER 1

# ᧐My Epiphany

## How Community Changed
## My Life

When I turned thirty, I realized I didn't belong. I was in my bathroom on a snowy Saturday in January in New York City, brushing my perpetually knotted hair and getting ready to go out, when I had an epiphany while looking at myself in the mirror: I didn't look happy.

Other than with my identical twin sister, Miki, and a small group of friends whom I loved but rarely saw because they were scattered around the globe, I didn't really feel a strong sense of belonging anywhere. I found myself stuck at the same sports bar every Saturday with friends who talked about stuff I didn't care about, and I frequently drank until I blacked out. I had just broken off an engagement, and I was not respecting myself or my body. And I was about to go out and do it all over again that night.

In that moment I knew something had to change. "What do I actually want?" I asked myself. "What matters to me? Is this what life's all about? Am I just a weekend warrior getting drunk with people who don't inspire me? Am I spending my time the way I want, or am I just numbing my loneliness and lack of deep connections?" I realized I was so tired of just c o a s t i n g.

Growing up, community had been at the center of my family's values. My parents immigrated to Canada in the 1970s— Dad is from India; Mom is from Japan. After meeting and falling in love in graduate school, they married and raised my sisters and me with little support from their families, who were thousands of miles away. Looking back, I now see how much they taught us about the importance of community, and how vulnerable and courageous they had to be to build their own community from scratch, especially with English as their second language.

You could say I've been part of a community since I was in my mother's womb, splishing and splashing around with my identical twin, Miki. My older sister, Yuri, was less than a year older than Miki and me (363 days older, to be exact), so from the very beginning I had

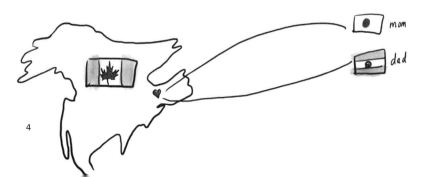

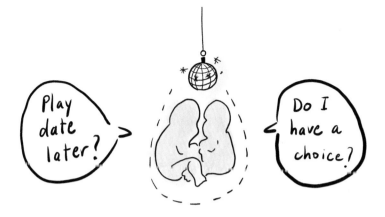

two sisters to play with, learn from, fight against, and make up with every day. It was always exciting—traumatic when we ganged up on one another and empowering when we stuck together.

Even when finances were tight, our parents threw the most amazing birthday celebrations and dinner parties, where we invented games for our friends and designed a signature fruit punch every year. I remember going downstairs to our basement during a party my dad threw for his engineering team and everyone was laughing at the dramatic poetry readings led by his British colleagues. All this stuck with me. Fun was very important in our family (once the copious amounts of chores and homework were completed, of course), and community organizing, including throwing events, has always been an integral way of life.

So when did that all change? How did I end up at thirty feeling like I didn't belong? I knew there had to be more to life.

Thinking back, I realized that for the past decade, I had placed making friends in the "if I have time" category. Work always came first and canceling on friends became normal. I spent time with people who were fine but not inspiring, just because it was easier. I would often delay or avoid the opportunity for a deeper connection with someone in real life because I wanted to catch up on social media. With Facebook and Instagram, I thought the more "friends" and "followers" I had, the better and more full my life would be. But it was more of an addiction, a rush, driven by ego, with insecurities bubbling up everywhere and offering very little satisfaction in the end. I was too proud (aka insecure) to reach out to potential new friends to see if anyone wanted to hang out, for fear of rejection. And I know now that I'm not alone in feeling these things. Being a thinking, feeling human is challenging—especially in the digital age!

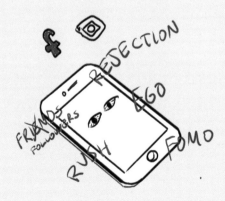

**MAYBE TURNING THIRTY WOKE ME UP,** but it really wasn't an "event" or a "low point" that I hit. It was a simple recognition. A realization. And I had to do something about it.

That night at the sports bar, I looked around and realized that almost everyone was avoiding their feelings the same way I had been.

People were looking around the room and not at one another. Half the bar was buried in their phones, and the other half was belligerently drunk and shouting at one another, grossly making out, or doing shots. I couldn't believe I had been a part of this and let it go on for so many years! I had nothing in common with these people! What was I thinking? I left my untouched beer and ran home with my head spinning, determined to make a change once and for all.

For the first time in my adult life, I was going to be intentional about my people.

As I grew more passionate about creating a community, I learned that isolation and a lack of belonging were becoming **A CRISIS:**

● One in four Americans report that they have ZERO friends to confide in and discuss important matters with; this number has tripled in the last thirty years, according to a 2006 study published in *American Sociological Review.*

● One in three Americans over the age of sixty-five is socially isolated; for those over the age of eighty-five, the number increases to one in two. This was heartbreaking to learn. The people who worked so hard to create the world we currently live in are being shoved into isolation instead of being celebrated?! I couldn't believe it!

● Another study found that having weak social ties is as harmful to our health as being an alcoholic and twice as harmful as obesity. Sit with that for a second: *Having poor social connections is as bad as being an alcoholic and twice as bad as being obese.*

● Another study found that isolation sets off a cellular chain reaction that increases inflammation and suppresses the body's autoimmune response to disease. We are sick from loneliness!

But then I learned about the "Blue Zones," the communities that live the longest—Okinawans in Japan, Sardinians in Italy, Costa Ricans, and Seventh-Day Adventists. They attribute their health and longevity to strong family ties, enjoyable social engagements, regular exercise, and eating mostly vegetables, usually in community.

This was a huge wake-up call. I had never realized how vital community was for my health and happiness. . . .

Becoming a social entrepreneur—a term used for people interested in creating a business that solves social, cultural, and environmental issues—is what ultimately opened my eyes to the importance of in-person communities. In 2010, I launched a children's nutrition education media company (à la *Sesame Street*) called Super Sprowtz to inspire kids to eat their vegetables. I wrote four children's books, produced fifty educational videos with the best puppeteers in the world, launched salad bar programs in underprivileged elementary schools across the country, and worked with some of the finest educators to create a comprehensive curriculum to make healthy eating fun, and we were impacting hundreds of thousands of kids around the world over the five years that I ran it. While we were making exciting strides, it was also the first time I saw how technology impacted the way kids connected with one another, as well as how it made them more sedentary and isolated.

During that period, in 2013, Miki, our friend Antonia, and I also launched THINX, an underwear technology company, with the intention of disrupting the market for feminine hygiene products. Our mission was not only to invent a new way to deal with menstruation (and serve the planet and the women in developing countries who lacked convenient solutions) but also to unify women and create a platform for women's empowerment. We spent three years tinkering with and developing our first prototype, and since our Kickstarter campaign in 2013, we've amassed an incredible community of hundreds of thousands of women who support THINX and our mission—which in turn has helped to reinforce my belief in the strength and importance of relationships across every aspect of life.

That same year (2013 was the year I kept saying YES!), my friend and coconspirator Matt and I came together over falafel late one night. Frustrated by how nightlife had become overrun by mean bouncers, too much alcohol, and digital divides, we wanted to get back to the basics of dancing and good, clean fun. What started out as a social experiment in which we gathered good friends in a basement lounge for early-morning yoga, dance, and merriment before going to work (several friends initially thought we were nuts!) has grown into Daybreaker, a mischievous movement that can now be found in twenty-five cities across the world and a dozen college campuses—with over 450,000 community members—and we're just getting started.

I now spend my days working as a Community Architect, a term I coined for myself and for all those who spend their days bringing humans together. The best architects think about materials, design, light and space, and Community Architects are no different. Communities are built, person by person, through thoughtful design and authentic, energetic connection points.

I've traveled all around the country and the world to launch Daybreaker, and throughout these travels I've sought out all sorts of people to talk to—students, teachers, engineers, hair stylists, entrepreneurs, psychologists, retirees, kids, taxi drivers, CEOs, you name it—in order to learn from the different communities that exist. I learned that many people think it's almost shameful to want to belong—they view it as "needy." Of course it's needy . . . it's a fundamental human need! On Maslow's hierarchy of basic human necessities, belonging sits right alongside the need for love.

# The need to belong is fundamental!

That said, since 1943, when Abraham Maslow first shared the concept for his hierarchy of needs, a lot has been discovered. Recent studies have shown that belonging affects not just our emotional well-being but our physical well-being too.* So I've updated Uncle Maslow's hierarchy to reflect that belonging is in fact a **basic human need** in the same category as food, water, touch, love, and shelter. I've also updated his hierarchy altogether to reflect our current belief systems and

*Maslow's Hierarchy of Needs, 1943*

new research findings. Here they are from the bottom up:

**Basic Human Needs:** Food, Water, Shelter, Belonging, Love, Positive Touch**

**Physical and Mental Well-Being:** Physical Health, Consensual Sex, Job, Home, Security, Presence, Cultivation of Curiosity

**Purpose:** Service Orientation, Finding Your Purpose on the Planet That Benefits Humankind (Parenting, Community)

**Joy:** Playfulness, Creativity, Wonder, Mindfulness—you have the satisfaction from a life of purpose to return to play, creativity, wonder and end suffering.

*The Harvard Study of Adult Development— 80-year study, 1938–present.

**Frank R. Wilson, *The Hand: How Its Use Shapes the Brain, Language, and Human Culture* (New York: Vintage Books, 1999).

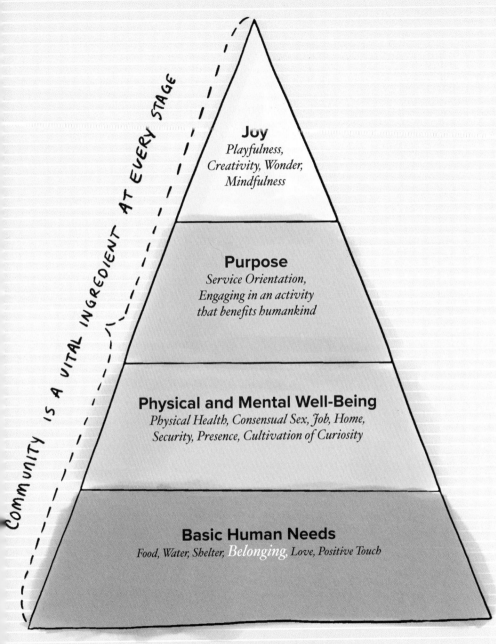

**Joy**
*Playfulness,
Creativity, Wonder,
Mindfulness*

**Purpose**
*Service Orientation,
Engaging in an activity
that benefits humankind*

**Physical and Mental Well-Being**
*Physical Health, Consensual Sex, Job, Home,
Security, Presence, Cultivation of Curiosity*

**Basic Human Needs**
*Food, Water, Shelter, Belonging, Love, Positive Touch*

COMMUNITY IS A VITAL INGREDIENT AT EVERY STAGE

*Agrawal's Hierarchy of Needs, 2017*

Across all four levels of my updated hierarchy of needs is one unifying ingredient: *community*. Without a community supporting you at each level, it's nearly impossible to move up the hierarchy. As psychologist Noam Shpancer wrote, "Human beings, fundamentally, are distinctly, spectacularly social. Lonely and isolated, we cannot survive, let alone thrive."

People often ask me, "How did you do it? How did you build these thriving communities?" These questions, along with my desire to synthesize what I learned through my personal and professional communities, inspired me to write this book. Sure, community and belonging can be squishy concepts, but I've identified several key principles and practices—all of which I continue to work on, both for myself and for the organizations I'm involved with—that have served me and hopefully will serve you too on your community building journey.

It took me two years to finally find my people, but when I did, every aspect of my life became more energizing, exciting, and full of possibilities. Of course there were (and are) many moments of learning along the way, but for the first time I felt safe to be fully me and to be celebrated for my individuality within a collective. Once I saw the power of community, and felt the deep joy it brought to me personally, it became my mission to help create community for others too.

Ultimately, my goal is to give you the blueprint to build and nurture your own community from scratch so that you find happiness, fulfillment, and success.

Let's GO!

# WHAT DO BELONGING AND COMMUNITY ACTUALLY MEAN?

To be human is to belong.
We were literally born in community,
attached to someone else.

I know, I know, we're frequently told to seek individuality and to be independent and strong, or to "go against the grain." This is all great—to a limit. Recognizing and honoring our unique qualities and authentic gifts is key to developing self-confidence. But *sharing* our unique gifts with the greater whole is vital to our humanity. Ultimately, humans are at the top of the food chain not because we are the strongest or fastest *individuals*— bears and cheetahs are much stronger and faster. We are at the top of the food chain because we are the best at *collaborating*, whether through storytelling, skill sharing, or community building. So let's honor our individuality and our authentic gifts by sharing ourselves with the world!

I define [BE·LONG·ING] as: a feeling of deep relatedness and acceptance; a feeling of "I would rather be here than anywhere else."

Belonging is the opposite of loneliness. It's a feeling of home, of "I can exhale here and be fully myself with no judgment or insecurity." Belonging is about shared values and responsibility, and the desire to participate in making your community better. It's about taking pride, showing up, and offering your unique gifts to others. *You can't belong if you only take.*

I define [COM·MU·NI·TY] as: a group of three or more people with whom you share similar values and interests and where you experience a sense of belonging.

Take a moment and sit with these definitions. Then let's move on.

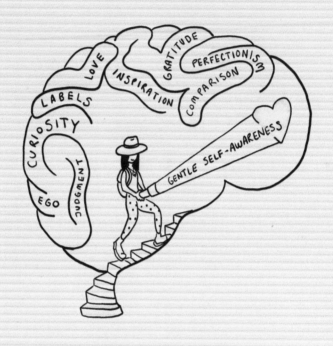

Gently, gently.
Always gently.

CHAPTER 2

# Gentle
# Self-Awareness

## How Are You Showing Up?

Y ou're probably asking, "OK, where do I start?!"
We are so quick to look outside of ourselves that we often
forget to Go IN and look under the hood. Building a
community where we feel a deep sense of belonging requires a real
and honest understanding of ourselves first. So let's take some real
time to Go *IN* and get cozy with ourselves before we Go *OUT*. There
are billions of people out there making up many different kinds of
communities—it can be overwhelming! By doing this work, you will
find the best community for *you*.

This chapter focuses on ***GENTLE SELF-AWARENESS***. We
are already such harsh critics of ourselves. When we work with *gentle*

self-awareness, the process of Going *IN* is much easier and kinder. Although it can feel intense at times to look inward, it can and should be a colorful and positive experience too. The goal is not to get *trapped* inside yourself by self-judgment, doubt, and regret—the goal is for you to become gently aware of who you are and intentional about what you want so that you can Go *OUT* and build your dream community.

My Community-Building Mantra

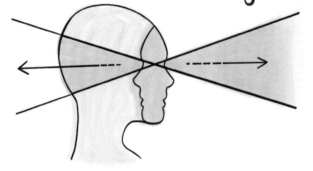

# You have to go in to go out.

## LET'S BEGIN BY GENTLY RECOGNIZING OUR PERSONAL HISTORY

We live in a time where we forget what we did yesterday, and our social media feeds race us through our lives.

**I decided to take a few hours one Sunday to slow down** and draw out a timeline of my life. I wore comfy pajamas, brought out the colored pens, drank about twelve cups of tea, and just . . . remembered. I recalled that I've moved eleven times (to new countries, cities, and neighborhoods), that I experienced 9/11 while living in NYC, that I've been through seven career changes and four major relationships.

I realized that seven of my biggest life moves happened in my twenties, when I was jumping around all over the country, and that it was during these times that I felt most out of my comfort zone. This exercise was instrumental in helping me see patterns in the choices I made. It also provided me with the clarity to recognize that it's always been up to me to choose which road to take and who to spend my time with—and that I get to keep doing that. We are so used to asking "what's next" in this world of twenty-four-hour news cycles that we can't even catch our breath! Let's take a moment to gently honor our history.

Recognizing all that got us here today and the events that shaped who we are will allow us to move forward with a clearer understanding of ourselves, what we want, and why.

# Radha's Life Timeline

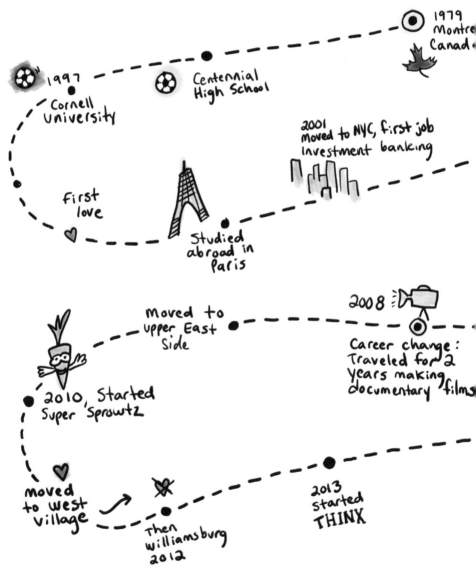

1979
Montre[al]
Canad[a]

1997
Cornell
University

Centennial
High School

2001
Moved to NYC, first job
Investment banking

First
love

Studied
abroad in
Paris

2008

Moved to
upper East
Side

Career change:
Traveled for 2
years making
documentary films

2010, Started
Super Sprowtz

moved
to West
village

Then
Williamsburg
2012

2013
started
THINK

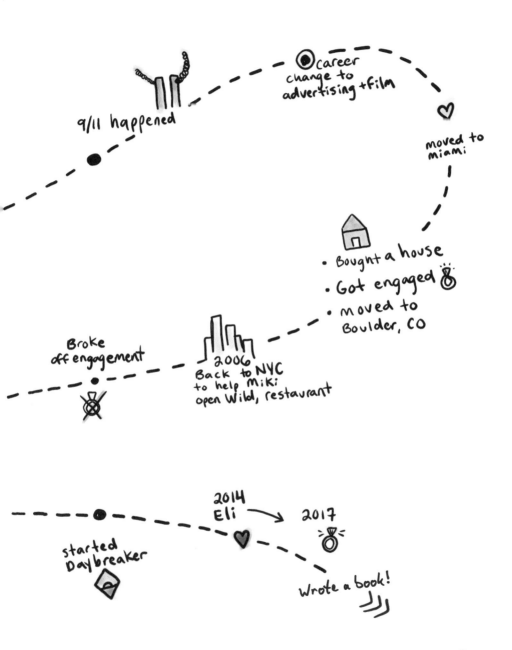

9/11 happened

career change to advertising + film

moved to miami

Bought a house

Got engaged

moved to Boulder, CO

Broke off engagement

2006 Back to NYC to help Miki open Wild, restaurant

started Daybreaker

2014 Eli

2017

Wrote a book!

# MAKE IT HAPPEN

**PLOT YOUR HISTORY.** Use this page to list all the cities you've lived in, the schools you've attended, the jobs you've had, the relationships you've been in, even the smaller life moments that only you remember. Add musical artists and albums that changed your life, movies that you've seen ten times, books you've reread. Include people who have had an impact on you, such as the teachers you loved. Get creative and break into your memory bank here! Start by writing down one thing, then keep going.

IN THE BEGINNING

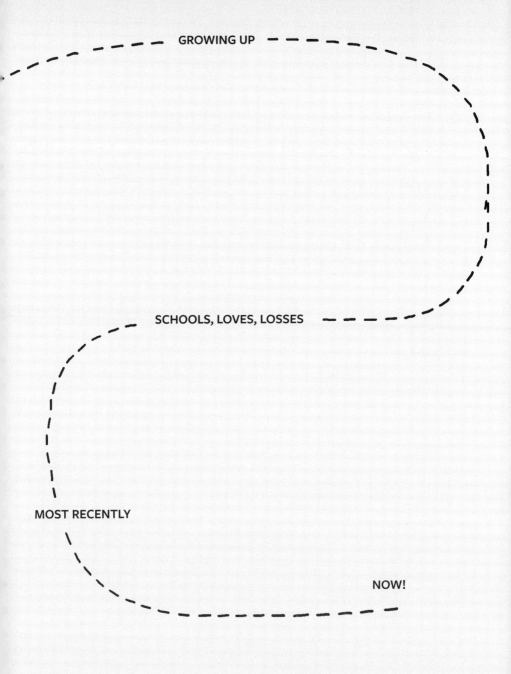

GROWING UP

SCHOOLS, LOVES, LOSSES

MOST RECENTLY

NOW!

# QUESTIONS TO ASK YOURSELF ONE BY ONE AFTER YOU'VE PLOTTED YOUR LIFE PATH:

1. Whom did you look up to?

..............................................................................

2. Whom did you depend on?

..............................................................................

3. Who kept you safe emotionally or physically? Who didn't?

..............................................................................

4. Who worried about you when you were feeling stressed?

..............................................................................

5. Whom did you take for granted?

..............................................................................

6. Did you choose your friends thoughtfully or did you fall into them?

..............................................................................

7. When were you running away?

..............................................................................

8. When have you played it safe?

..............................................................................

9. When did you make excuses?

.................................................................................................................................

.................................................................................................................................

10. When did you feel most alive and fist-pumping in life?

.................................................................................................................................

.................................................................................................................................

.................................................................................................................................

11. Where have you struggled?

.................................................................................................................................

.................................................................................................................................

.................................................................................................................................

12. What part of your past do you want to forgive?

.................................................................................................................................

.................................................................................................................................

.................................................................................................................................

13. What more do you need?

.................................................................................................................................

.................................................................................................................................

.................................................................................................................................

Sit with your history and get really honest with it. Remember to be gentle with yourself, and without judgment. Imagine your younger self and speak tenderly to her or him. The time you take to get gently aware of your journey thus far will help you see your path forward with more clarity.

Consider doing this exercise with a friend, in a class, or with family members. Sharing it with people you trust can reveal more about you—and them. If you're open to sharing your history with me, I want to see it! Take a photo of your timeline and share it on Instagram @love.radha and #belongbook.

## LET'S TALK ABOUT EGO

**Imagine a** *Green Ego* **and a** *Red Ego*. Each one sits on a shoulder, whispering into your ear. Their existence and what they whisper to you is fueled by your history and life experiences.

One keeps you moving forward and the other slows you down. Your Green Ego stands up for you and wants the best for you. It maintains your self-esteem and operates from a place of abundance. Your Green Ego is driven and passionate and pushes you to achieve in positive ways. Your Green Ego is your biggest cheerleader.

Your Red Ego is just as present on your other shoulder, but its intentions are not the same. Your Red Ego is afraid. It holds you back and makes you judge yourself and the world. It makes you a bad listener and scared of being wrong. It is not self-aware and is always trying to prove itself. Your Red Ego is self-centered and hides behind overconfidence. Your Red Ego bottles things up, doesn't share when it needs help, and hides behind pride.

Be Gently Self-Aware of when your Green and Red Egos are present. Notice them. That's all.

# MAKE IT HAPPEN

Whenever you're having a **Red Ego** or **Green Ego** moment this week, write down what they're whispering to you. It's eye opening!

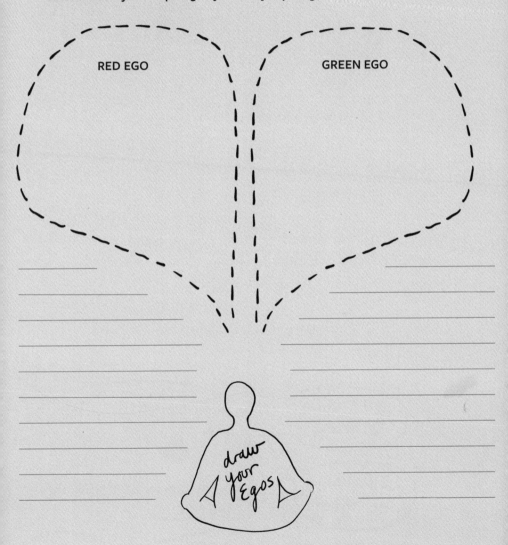

RED EGO

GREEN EGO

draw your Egos

# THE MEAN GIRLS OF YOUR MIND

## Let's Talk About Comparison, Perfectionism, and Judgment

*Comparison, Perfectionism, and Judgment are BFFs.*

Comparison, Perfectionism, and Judgment are the Mean Girls of your mind. (Mean Girls can also be Mean Guys—they come in all shapes, genders, and sizes.) They bully your authentic self, make you feel insecure, and pull you away from who you really are. They're egocentric and care only about themselves, even though they're driven by what others are doing and saying. Comparison separates. Judgment disapproves. Perfectionism nitpicks.

They are often responsible for our anxiety. They condition us to judge everything we think and do. They whisper to us . . .

When we follow them, we drift farther away from our authentic selves and start focusing all our attention on what *others* are doing and whether they're doing it better than us or if they're doing it right. Because these Mean Girls can be loud and powerful in our minds, we are quick to criticize, blame, judge, and discard, and we focus on the negative things about ourselves and others. Here's the thing: Mean Girls never go away. They're always around. It's up to you to decide whether you want to sit with them at lunch or if you want to walk past them and focus on the table with all the kids who are welcoming, curious, warm, fun, and open-minded.

## Social Media on Perfectionism and Judgment

Social media has made the Mean Girls very powerful because we now have ways to compare and judge ourselves at every moment of every day.

We also have filters and tools that play into our need for perfection as we take our perfectly angled selfies, endlessly edit our photos, and spend too much time writing clever captions. Appearing to be perfect can actually be intimidating and scary for others and can make it hard to be approachable—it's tough to relate to someone who projects perfection! Our weird quirks and unique qualities make us relatable. *Who defines perfection anyway?* The media? Magazines? Your peers? Your family? Instagram influencers? There's nothing more approachable (and refreshing!) than being flawed and being OK about it.

Mean Girls inspire vanity and insecurity instead of community and support. According to a University of Michigan study published in 2013, the more time people spend on social media, the less happy

they feel about their own lives. They also experience
a decreased sense of belonging and end up
spending more time with the Mean Girls, judging,
comparing, and nitpicking. When I scrolled
through social media and saw friends posting
highlights from their lives, even if I wanted to
be happy for them—even if I *was* happy for
them—I'd still feel a twinge of the Mean Girl
mind-set. I'd compare myself to my friends
and judge each post they put up. It's hard, if
not impossible, to get Mean Girls to leave
the cafeteria of our minds completely. The best advice is to gently
recognize when they're taking over and start moving your awareness
and thoughts toward a space of support, curiosity, and excitement.
Then walk on by.

# Meet Your Soul Sisters

## Let's Talk About Inspiration, Gratitude, and Curiosity

*Inspiration, Gratitude, and Curiosity are BFFs.*

Your **Soul Sisters** (or Soul Brothers or Soul Family) are Inspiration, Gratitude, and Curiosity. They sit two tables down from the Mean Girls. You'll always have to walk past the Mean Girls' table—and make a conscious decision to keep walking past them as they call out to you—but once you've made it past their table, you'll realize that the Soul Sisters are even more powerful. Once you sit with them, you'll want to eat lunch with them every single day, because they make you feel good! They're welcoming, thoughtful, curious, and grateful for each person sitting at the table. Everyone around them feels listened to and acknowledged. They're the ones everyone in school goes to when they're having a crisis. They are all *you*! It's up to you to gently move your awareness from a negative space to a positive space. Here's what would happen:

**Comparison** → **Inspiration**

Instead of comparing yourself to someone else, you allow them to inspire you.

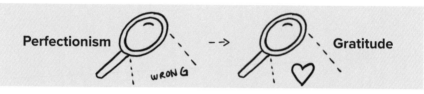

**Perfectionism** → **Gratitude**

Instead of nitpicking everything that's going "wrong," you focus your awareness on all the things that are going right and feel grateful for those things.

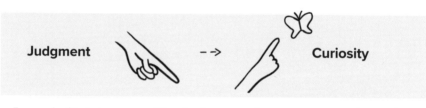

**Judgment** → **Curiosity**

Instead of judging yourself and others, you become curious about why you feel judgmental in the first place and move your awareness toward a place of curiosity: "Why do I feel this way? Why am I judging this person? Why am I judging myself in this way? Can I learn more about this rather than judge it?" Curiosity will set you free.

Still, in so many areas of my life, I continue to catch myself sitting with the Mean Girls that cause stress and frustration—how I judge my body, my friendships, and my romantic relationships;

how I appear in public; how I talk and present myself to others; my online status updates; and how I'm being perceived. Of course it's exhausting—and anxiety-inducing! Those Mean Girls are MEAN!

One of the most insightful stories I've heard about the Soul Sisters came from my friend and colleague Ryan, who battled depression for most of his teen years. His therapist helped him eradicate his depression with one simple idea: *curiosity*.

She showed him that he was operating from a place of finality— "This is it, I'm depressed for life"—and helped him move his mind-set to one of curiosity—"Hm, what *is* this feeling? Is there another way to see this? What else is out there?" Once he practiced this shift in his mind-set—it changed everything.

Keep going back to your Soul Sisters and spend lots of time with them. They will help you live the life you want.

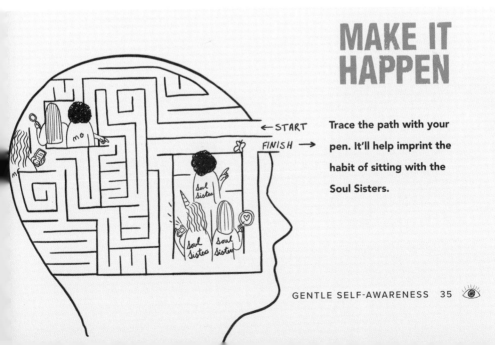

## MAKE IT HAPPEN

←START
FINISH →

Trace the path with your pen. It'll help imprint the habit of sitting with the Soul Sisters.

# How to walk past the Mean Girls and continue to navigate the cafeteria of your mind

# MAKE IT HAPPEN

Practice daily gratitude while brushing your teeth. Think of three things you're grateful for. It could be as simple as the soft sheets on your bed or a sunny day. This has been a game changer for me. Trust me—I rolled my eyes when this exercise was first suggested to me, but it actually works. After a few days, you'll feel the positive effects. **#tryit**

 I allow myself fifteen minutes per day on social media to post, scroll, and comment. I use a timer and am aware of when I'm comparing myself versus when I'm being inspired. **#waymorefun**

I removed the Facebook app from my phone and use it only on the web. **#gamechanger**

I recognize when I'm having a Mean Girl Moment (MGM) and really focus on walking past them toward my Soul Sisters. I'll say to myself,  "Radha, MGM," and grow curious about why I was feeling that way in the first place. More often than not, we judge others based on our own insecurities. Again, curiosity will set you free.

When I'm waiting for a friend, I don't go straight to social media on my phone to distract myself (which can end up in a Mean Girl Moment). Instead I think about the friend who's coming and all the ways I want to connect with him or her.

Chances are you're going to have the opportunity to do one of these things today. So try it!

# MAKE IT HAPPEN

All this work we're doing on Gentle Self-Awareness is preparing us to be happier humans and to be able to find and build our dream community.

Put a photo of yourself as a little kid— preferably one where you're laughing and free—inside your medicine cabinet. Each time you open your medicine cabinet, think of three things you're grateful for.

Wrap a ribbon around your toothbrush to remind yourself to be grateful for three things each time you brush your teeth.

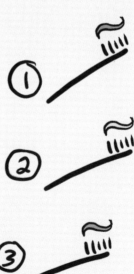

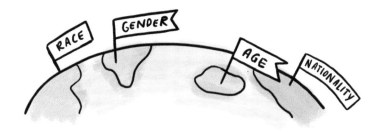

## LET'S TALK ABOUT LABELS

**As humans, we are natural storytellers. We especially tell ourselves stories.**

We have spent thousands of years organizing ourselves into simple labels so we can better understand the wildly complex environment we live in. We have figured out how to view one another by seeing nationality, race, gender, sexual orientation, socioeconomic background, political orientation, education, religion, age group, and on and on.

We have also labeled ourselves and others through our behaviors and attitudes—social, antisocial, honest, kind, liar, manipulative, gentle, aggressive, funny, serious, etc.

Labels work best when we use them to better understand ourselves *as we relate to one another*. For example, when my friend Amber told me that she connects better one-on-one than in larger groups, she wasn't separating herself—she was giving me clues in order to better connect with her. Knowing this, I didn't label her as antisocial. In fact, just the opposite! But too often we use labels not to connect, but to separate. We misunderstand them, and they make us more isolated, anxious, and stressed than before we took on the label.

# I am all these things,

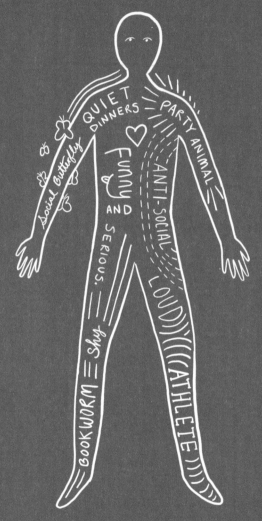

# not just one.

When I hear terms like "introvert" and "extrovert" (Jung, I'm looking at you!), I cringe. It's such an oversimplification of who we are—it feels like a one-size-fits-all statement. We subscribe to these labels as truths without any further inquiry and then simply "band together" under one label and stop actually listening to one another (hello, politics and religion). We are far more complex and interesting than any label!

Here's what I do know: Every single human is uniquely different, and at each moment we *feel* something different. It's unfair to label ourselves as one certain type of person, because it creates a self-fulfilling prophecy. I may be feeling annoyed or happy or irrational on the day I take a personality test, and then I'm forever labeled as that kind of person, so I *become* that person. In addition, I may have some behaviors and triggers that only come out under certain circumstances and are not present in many, or even most, parts of my life.

The important thing to note here is that if you *do* feel compelled to label yourself as a certain "type" of person, remember that the goals for labeling are to better understand ourselves as *we relate to one another*—not to better represent yourself, not to better understand someone else, and not to give yourself an "out" because there's something you just don't like doing.

# Let's label to connect with one another, not label to separate!

Jung himself said that "there is no such thing as a pure introvert or extrovert. Such a person would be in a lunatic asylum."

All this is to say we all exist on a *spectrum* between the two polarities. I call this spectrum **Metavert**. **We are all Metaverts.**

# Remember: Life is not as absolute as we often make it.

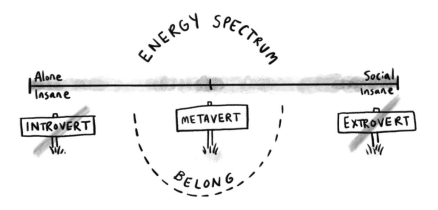

# MAKE IT HAPPEN

**Be gently aware of your self-labeling and your labeling of others and ask yourself if it's separating or connecting you to others.**

## LET'S TALK ABOUT BINGEING

As animals, humans are wired to binge when given the opportunity. "Consume as much as you can in case there's no more tomorrow!" Marketers and advertisers have quickly figured this out and push us to binge as often and as much as possible. We binge eat sugar, meat, fat, and carbs, taxing our bodies and shortening our lives; we binge drink alcohol, causing both physical and emotional repercussions; we binge on the internet, spending an average of ten hours per day on screens swiping and scrolling*; we binge shop for "more stuff!" polluting our planet; and binge watch eight episodes in a row—and then wonder why we are so stressed, anxious, lethargic, or depressed!

When I was in college, I really felt the pressure to drink. I hated it and loved it at the same time. Drinking made me feel less insecure, but I was often out of control, on edge, and overly emotional the next day. Then getting drunk became what we did almost *every weekend*. Why did everything have to revolve around alcohol? I became a different version of myself and attracted the wrong friends.

Ultimately, bingeing *never feels good.* It never ends well. It's numbing and anxiety inducing.

*Nielsen Total Audience Report, Q1 2016.

**HAVE YOU HEARD ABOUT THE "ATTENTION ECONOMY"?** It's where companies fight for our attention. The more content we binge on, the more money these companies make, so they're motivated to keep us glued to our phones and computers. The ethos of the "greater whole" and "community first" is trumped by profit interests and wanting us to watch more videos, click on more baity headlines, and share it with our friends. Bingeing is profitable!

## LET'S TALK ABOUT YOUR HUMAN MACHINE

Now let's consider our amazing human machines (aka our bodies), which work so hard to keep us alive, yet we don't always pay attention to them. Sometimes when you're feeling all the emotional things, it's really nothing more than you're hungry, you haven't slept, you have seasonal affective disorder and need some vitamin D, you're PMS-ing, you're cold, you're stressed at work with too much on your plate, etc. We are different people every day based on a host of variables, and our emotional well-being is deeply intertwined with our physical body. Let's notice how our magical machine is feeling and how we're treating it before we start calling ourselves names, telling stories, and labeling and isolating ourselves.

# MAKE IT HAPPEN

Be gently aware of how bingeing plays a role in your life and write down all the areas in which you think you may binge. Ask yourself how it's affecting your emotional well-being and your relationships.

.......................................................................................................................

.......................................................................................................................

.......................................................................................................................

.......................................................................................................................

.......................................................................................................................

.......................................................................................................................

.......................................................................................................................

Be gently aware of how your magical human machine is doing and make a habit of checking in with your physical self.

❏ SLEEPY

❏ HUNGRY

❏ PMS-ING

❏ STRESSING

❏ FEELING COLD/HOT

❏ OTHER

## WHAT'S IN YOUR BACKPACK?

Now imagine your colorful rainbow—your history, Egos, Mean Girls, Soul Sisters, labels, bingeing—all tucked into an imaginary backpack that you wear every day. Then imagine that every person walking down the street has their own backpack filled with *their* history, *their* emotional stuff that makes them uniquely *them*. What if, when someone is mean or comes across as harsh or abrasive, we considered "What's in their backpack?" We could learn about their colorful rainbow instead of judging them and getting upset or frustrated. I believe we would be more loving, more empathetic, and more gently aware.

## Our Gentle Awareness Prepares Us to Be Intentional

All the exercises we've done so far on Gentle Self-Awareness and observing our colorful spectrum are helping us learn about ourselves so that we become more comfortable and confident with who we are. Our gentle recognition makes us more *Intentional*. Intention is about being thoughtful and purposeful about what you want.

Take your time with this chapter and all the things you're discovering about yourself. When you see and interact with others this week, imagine that they all have Green and Red Egos sitting on their shoulders talking to them and that they're trying to decide whether to sit with the Mean Girls or the Soul Sisters in their mind's cafeteria. Our gentle awareness makes us more empathetic to ourselves and to each other.

Gently process it, observe it, and then let's move on.

When you are intentional,
the world unlocks
in your favor.

# CHAPTER 3

# ᑫntention

## Write It Down and Dig Deep

Now that we are gently self-aware of our colorful rainbow, we're going to dig deep and get intentional.

## Intention is about being thoughtful and purposeful about what we want.

Once we become more clear about what we're really interested in and actually want, we can Go OUT and create our dream community.

## FIRST LET'S ASSESS OUR VALUES, INTERESTS, AND ABILITIES (VIA)

Typically we do this kind of "assessment" around our Values, Interests, and Abilities (VIA) for our professional lives. When I first graduated from college and moved to New York City in 2001 (two months before 9/11), I got a job as an analyst at an investment bank on Wall Street. When I went through the interview process (and bought the only pantsuit I would ever own), I had to answer so many questionnaires and go through nine grueling interviews over the course of several months. They asked me brainteasers, probed about my life and my family, and asked what movies I liked to watch. We also went to many lunches and dinners with the other candidates to "get to know one another." Before I got an offer, the human resources department did a full background check, and scrutinized me for culture fit, analytical thinking, and professionalism (boy, did I fool them on that one!). While it was both exhilarating and as invasive as a proctology exam, I was impressed by the thoroughness.

Then I began thinking: Why don't we conduct similar HR practices for our personal lives?

Why don't we ask ourselves if our friends are a "good fit" for us based on our *personal* values, interests, and abilities.

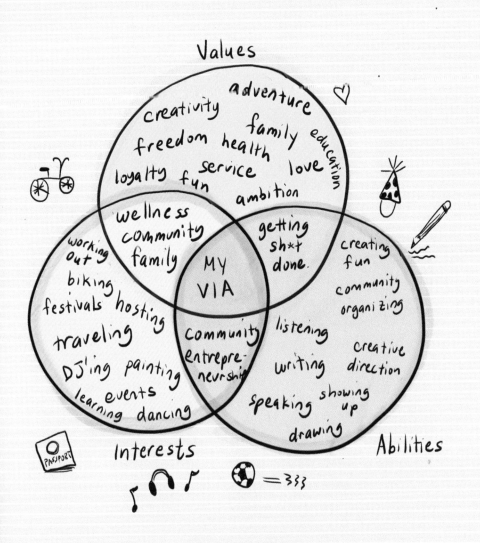

Values

creativity adventure ♡
family
freedom health education
loyalty service love
fun
ambition

wellness getting creating
community sh*t fun
family done. community
organizing

MY
VIA

working
out community listening
biking entrepre- creative
festivals hosting neurship writing direction
traveling speaking showing
DJ'ing painting up
learning events drawing
dancing

Interests Abilities

⚽ = 333

*Radha's VIA, 2017*

And why not ask what VIAs we can offer our community? When I finally did this exercise through the lens of my friendships and community at age thirty, I realized that the friends I was hanging out with in my twenties did not align with my personal VIA. Their interests were beer, football, and dating (totally get it!), while mine were dancing, music festivals, dinner parties, painting, and dreaming up my next big idea. They liked to plan; I loved spontaneous adventures. They liked to go to the same place every weekend and have a "local joint," while I wanted to explore and do something totally different every weekend. They loved the stability of their full-time jobs, and I wanted the excitement of starting my own business. As a result, I felt out of sync and didn't feel a strong sense of belonging when I was with them. It was nobody's fault! I was just going along for the ride and was never *intentional* about my community.

If we don't take the time to do a Personal VIA assessment for ourselves, we may end up in relationships that deplete us and in misaligned communities that don't serve us.

Fill out your Personal VIA. See the following pages for examples of values, interests, and abilities. Take your time with this. Knowing your true VIA is vital to finding and creating your dream community

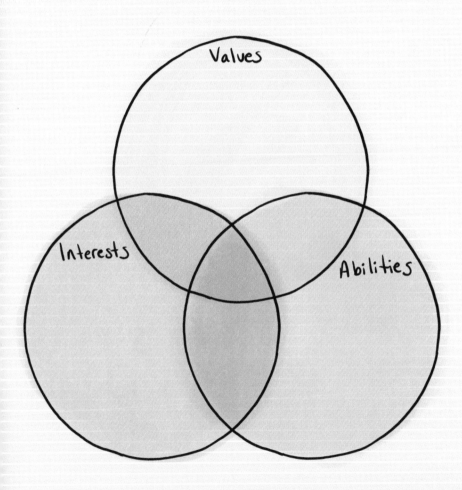

## Values

Dig deep and ask yourself what matters to you. What is truly important in your life? Are success, wealth, and recognition important to you? Love, trust, and leadership? Spirituality, balance, and autonomy? There are no wrong answers. Values are the lens through which you judge what's important. They help you determine your "Personal Core Values," or your non-negotiables in life, and how you want to spend your precious time.

### EXAMPLES OF VALUES

Yours may not be on this list, so take your time and dig deep!

achievement

authenticity

boldness

compassion

creativity

curiosity

determination

fairness

faith

fame

fun

growth

happiness

humor

Inner Harmony

kindness

knowledge

leadership

learning

loyalty

meaningful work

patience

popularity

recognition

religion

reputation

respect

silliness

spirituality

stability

peace

thoughtfulness

wealth

wisdom

## Interests

Values are more intrinsic—part of the nature of who you are as a person—whereas interests are more tangible. Think about everything that interests you. Here are some suggestions:

painting

hiking

yoga

video games

start-ups

stock market

traveling

learning new languages

food

working out

chess

designing

blogging

surfing

self-improvement

photography

documentaries

dancing

building things

watching Disney movies

knitting

cooking

filmmaking

scuba diving

marine biology

earth sciences

recycling

community service

faith/church

skill sharing

music festivals

adventure travel

poetry

glassblowing

reading

writing

taking baths

homemaking

hosting dinners

meditation

playing music

space exploration

technology

artificial intelligence

# What are you interested in?
# What are you passionate about?

Write these things down in your Interests circle. Name **at least five interests, fifteen at most**. Some people like to go deep on a few interests, while others like to dabble in many things.

## Abilities

There can be quite a bit of overlap between interests and abilities, but this circle stands for all the skills you can bring to your community. Can you cook like a champ? Do you excel at organizing people? Do you make others laugh? Are you good at getting someone to see another perspective? Do you enjoy cleaning? We often take all of our abilities as humans for granted. Grabbing things with your opposable thumbs is an ability! An ability is often a skill you don't think of as a skill. I have a friend who has a green thumb—every plant she cares for survives and thrives. My partner, Eli, loves cooking and always creates elaborate meals for our community, while I'd rather host (and eat!). My brother-in-law Andrew has spent years honing his conversation game. He's candid about his social anxiety and believes that asking thoughtful questions opens people up and makes him and the other person feel more comfortable in a conversation. That's a skill! What comes naturally to me is igniting new ideas, bringing people together, designing experiences, and connecting dots—but I didn't realize these were "abilities" until I started my entrepreneurial journey.

So what are your skills and abilities? If you don't think you have any, think again. Give it some thought. Consider the compliments or gratitude you've received for things you've done. It could be as simple as being prepared and showing up with something to share. Write them all down. Community is built on sharing our gifts and abilities with the greater whole. List what comes naturally to you as well as skills you've worked on over the years.

# Every one of us has something to contribute, from emotional support to organizational skills and beyond.

## THE THREE COLUMNS

The morning after I left the sports bar that snowy January Saturday and decided to get intentional about my community, I sat down at my kitchen counter, hair disheveled, and grabbed my favorite Moleskine notebook (you know, the one that makes you feel creative) and neatly drew out a three-column list. These three columns would become the beginning of my journey into a true community.

Column one became a list of everything I was looking for in a friend. I wanted friends who talked about ideas and not one another, who were ambitious game changers, who liked adventure and fun, who showed up and took care of one another, who went to the gym and took care of themselves, who were interest*ing* and interest*ed*. I wanted friends who *listened*.

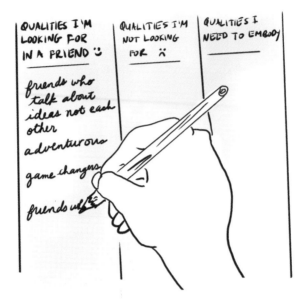

Column two featured all the qualities I *didn't* want in a friend: shit-talkers, drama queens, negative Nancies, alcoholics, too-cool-for-schools, shoulder-shruggers, and lazies (you know what I mean!).

Column three, probably the most important column, was for all the qualities *I* needed to embody in order to attract the friends that I wanted—I needed to be a better listener, less of a workaholic, and more accountable, as well as less critical and more forgiving.

I had never done anything like this before—taken the time to write down what I was looking for in a *friend*. Who does that?!

Up until then, I had stumbled into friend groups and fallen into communities. After all, that's how it worked when we were in elementary school and high school. The person in our homeroom became our best friend. Proximity was everything. Growing up, I had never experienced a world in which we could actually *choose* our own ideal friends who served and inspired us. Or was I just never taught to think this was a possibility?

The next week I brought my Moleskine with me everywhere I went. I refined my three-column list while riding the subway, in between meetings, and on the elliptical at the gym.

It was cathartic and SO exciting. I had finally taken my life into my own hands. I was going to seek out my community and build it myself.

When I did my three columns, the last column really opened my eyes to my own behaviors and patterns. I was attracting the wrong friends because I wasn't fully showing up as myself. It all came down to the *energy* I was putting out into the world and what it was sending back to me.

**Let's start with column one:**

This is where you write down every single quality you're looking for in a friend or in your community. Pull some words from your Values circle. It can be any quality you want: funny, health-conscious, creative, passionate, kind, silly, creative, smart, likes the outdoors, exercises, loves dancing, talks about big ideas, asks questions, says "Yes!" with an exclamation point, likes electronic music, wears striped socks, enjoys avocados, watches documentaries. Write it ALL down. You can create this list for your romantic partner too, but let's go through this exercise through the lens of what you want in a friend or community first. It's not always the same! Even if you're married or in a serious relationship, community is still vital for your happiness!

**On to column two:**

This is for listing all the qualities you're NOT looking for in a friend or community. This could be: spends all weekend watching sports, is a couch potato, hurts people's feelings, a shoulder-shrugger, shit-talker,

MAKE IT
HAPPEN

| QUALITIES I'M LOOKING FOR IN A FRIEND | QUALITIES I'M NOT LOOKING FOR IN A FRIEND | QUALITIES I NEED TO EMBODY |
| --- | --- | --- |
| | | |

negative Nelly, jealous, envious, angry person, binge-drinker, bad listener. It can also include things that aren't necessarily bad, but just aren't for you, such as someone who's not self-aware, or wants to hang back and comment instead of participate.

**Column three is the one that can really change your life:**

This includes all the qualities *you* want to embody in order to attract the friends that you want. This is your time to be gently honest with yourself about how you're showing up. Are you a shit-talker? A workaholic? A bad listener? Quick to anger? Do you troll the internet? Are you lazy or selfish or bossy? Do you hang out with the Mean Girls a lot? It's OK! We've all been there. I didn't realize how flaky I was until I was named "Most likely to triple book" at our annual holiday party. #wakeupcall

Here are some examples for column three:

"I want to be a better listener; I want to show up fully at get-togethers and not be on my phone; I want to relax on the booze because I get drunk too fast; I want to walk past the Mean Girls and be less negative and judgmental; I want to be less of a workaholic and not cancel on my friends; I want to be more empathetic; I want to be more patient; I want to add more value to my relationships; I want to work out more and feel better about myself."

Use "I want" statements when you're writing your list down instead of "I need to." These are qualities you're intentionally seeking out. You don't *need* to be this way. You're *choosing* to go down this path—and you will be revisiting these qualities as your Values, Interests, and Abilities evolve too—what you're interested in today may be totally different a few years from now. Give yourself room to grow!

# MAKE IT HAPPEN

Sit with your VIA (Values, Interests, Abilities) and your three columns and gently observe how you feel about them. We will be coming back to this later on in the book. If you're open to sharing (it can be anonymous), snap a pic and tag @love.radha and #belongbook.

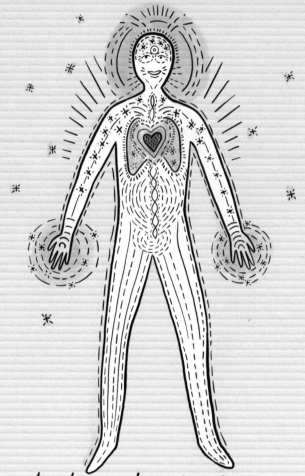

Once you truly understand that you
are just beautiful energy wrapped in
human form, your fear and "otherness"
will disappear and you will experience
deep belonging and fellowship.

# CHAPTER 4

# ℰnergy

## Set the Temperature, Why FYFs Are Friend Magnets, and How to Release Your Natural D.O.S.E.

I realized a long time ago that energy, enthusiasm, and excitement matter. *Really* matter. Good people want to hang out, work, travel, and do business with people who use exclamation points (literally or metaphorically) and who say "F*ck yeah! I'm IN!" to life. Positive energy is contagious. Shoulder-shruggers are often left behind.

Every day of our lives we absorb, mirror, and emit energy all around us. As evolved animals, it's our most potent form of communication. I spent my twenties unaware of how much I was mirroring and absorbing other people's energies, and when I turned thirty, I looked at myself in the mirror and didn't recognize the person

I saw. My energy was muted, my fire was dim. Our energy defines us, and the people we surround ourselves with help shape our energy. Our romantic partners, work colleagues, and friends, and outside forces like the news and politics—even the barista down the street—can affect our energy every day. It's either energizing or depleting. How

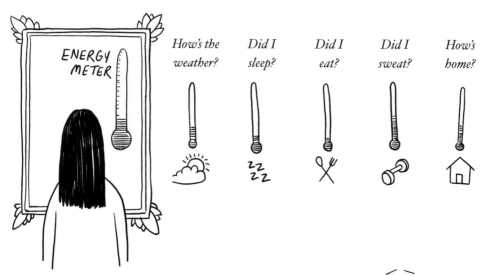

we take care of our bodies, our incredible "human meat suits" (as my friend Mark likes to call our human form), including what we eat, how much we exercise, and how much we sleep, affects our energy levels too.

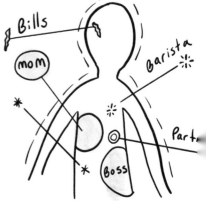

# Energy of Meeting for the First Time

Energy is felt the moment we meet another person. Our eyes and our demeanor do the talking for us. It's our very first impression. How we look or dress matters far less than the energy we emit to the world.

Over the last several years, I've sat down with leadership coaches, CEOs, psychologists, politicians, matchmakers, professors, yoga teachers, athletic coaches, energy healers, and musicians to learn about their practices, and each expert said, unsolicited and with certainty, that the main characteristic they look for in any relationship is *energy*—they just had different words for it:

# Vibration * Spark Spirit * Attitude * Presence *

All these conversations confirmed for me that energy is the most potent human attribute available to us, and we need to pay close attention to it. As a Community Architect, understanding and curating energy is my most valuable skill.

Energy defines how we feel and how others perceive us more than any other quality. It powerfully shapes community and our sense of belonging. My Indian father calls it "wibes" ("vibes"). The first thing he would always say when he met any new love interest that my sisters and I brought home was "he has good wibes" or "bad wibes." Then his eyes would flash in either a friendly or scary way and we knew immediately how the weekend was going to go. Begrudgingly, I'll admit he was most often right.

Energy is a great equalizer in life.
It doesn't matter what you do
for a living or
how much money you have—
the energy you put out is the energy
you get back.
Negative energy breeds
negative community.
Positive energy breeds positive
community.
It's that simple.

# So What Is ENERGY Anyway?

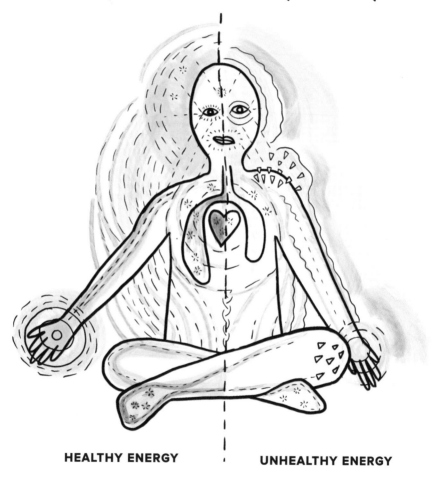

HEALTHY ENERGY          UNHEALTHY ENERGY

Energy is the invisible backbone of our lives. It controls the way we see the world, and how others perceive us. It quietly shapes our daily existence. It also controls our physical health—when we're stressed, hurt, or angry we often become physically rigid; we forget to breathe and heal more slowly compared to when our energy is positive and happy, our muscles are relaxed, and we breathe easily.

Most days we fluctuate between high energy and low energy based on a host of variables—physical conditions (health, fitness, nutrition, sleep), emotional conditions (our current relationships, how we were raised), seasonal and weather conditions, or time of day.

Take a moment to gently recognize how much your *Energy Meter* fluctuates throughout your day.

# Do you wish you had more energy? Do you wish you could relax more? How are you taking care of yourself? Are you exercising? Are you eating well?

Take some time to think about how full or empty your tank is most days and what you're doing to energize yourself.

Energy is our most important internal and external force field to monitor every single day. It starts from deep within our cells and radiates out through our eyes, our pores, our gestures, our speech, our smile, our yells, screams, and every expression and emotion in between. Energy comes in all shapes.

# ENERGY

Your energy is felt by those around you, and it is within your power to control and change it at any given moment with your thoughts and actions.

## LAME ENERGY

While our energy is in our control, it takes awareness to change it. Every day we are pushed and tricked by marketers and advertisers to pour our energy toward what I call the Look-at-Me-Economy, or *LAME* (let's call a spade a spade, folks), where we're taught that "likes" and "followers" are more valuable than human-to-human

# Cycle of Ding Addiction

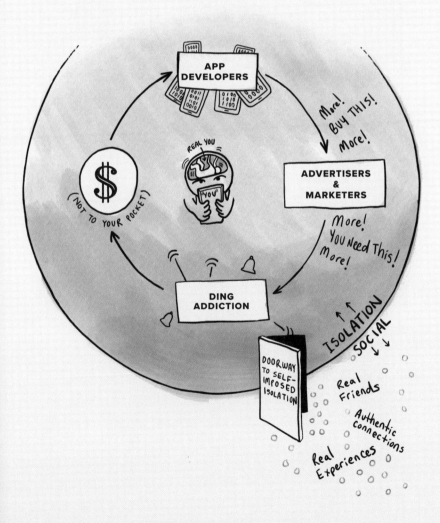

interactions. Billions of dollars are spent every year to understand human psychology and ways to keep us glued to our devices.

*Road to Isolation*

# We've become addicted to the dopamine rush that fires from our brains every time we get a new "like" or notification.

Dopamine is one of the "happy" brain chemicals that releases when you feel pleasure due to a reward—imagine a slot machine in Vegas and the excitement you feel when you're pulling the handle in anticipation of three sevens. It's the same brain chemical that gets released when you hear a ding from your phone or an app in anticipation of a new message—and boy is it addictive. Because we're becoming increasingly addicted to the dopamine hits we get from our phones, we're becoming less interested in pursuing deeper relationships (which ultimately make us happier) in favor of surface-level ones that help us gain more followers to feed our "ding addiction." It's a vicious cycle led by app developers, marketers, and advertisers, and one we have to *actively* (NOT gently!) get out of.

## AXIS OF ENERGY

Now that you have a clear understanding of the vital importance of energy, write down a list of everyone you currently spend time with. Organize your list by school, work, family, friends, romantic relationships, sports teams, and anyone else you see frequently.

We are going to assess your energy and the energy of those you surround yourself with on the graph on the following page. I call it your Axis of Energy. Once you've organized your list, go through each of the axes on the graph and start plotting your chart. I like using different colors for different groups (i.e., a red pen for work colleagues, a blue pen for friends, a green pen for family, etc.).

## ENERGY AWARENESS

Doing this exercise will help you identify your energy patterns. You may realize, "Wow! Everyone I surround myself with is super inauthentic and low energy! No wonder I'm so negative and low energy too!" or "I haven't been focusing on self-care, so my energy is low and it's making me negative and stressed," or "I really want to set a goal for myself to focus on being more high energy and positive." Once you have your list of people, you can place them on the axis. Here's how . . .

# Axis of Energy

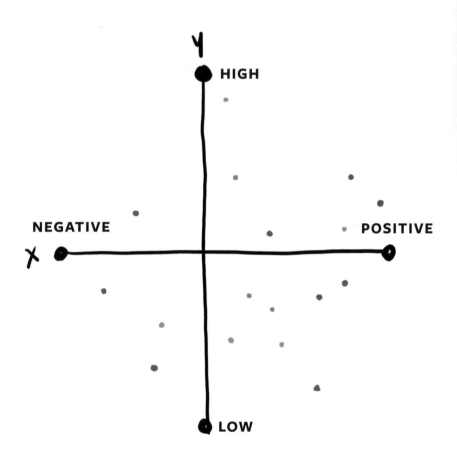

© 2017 RADHA AGRAWAL

**The x-axis**, which runs left to right, represents how people affect you when you are with them. There are people who affect you negatively (toward the left) and positively (toward the right). That may change from day to day, but we're looking for an overall feeling you get when you're with them. You know what it feels like to be with someone who makes you feel good. That's positive energy. You also probably know what negative energy feels like. It's not always mean or bad—it can also mean hurt or scared energy.

**The y-axis**, running up and down, is High and Low energy. This represents the kind of liveliness or vitality that people transmit. You know when someone is generally enthusiastic, interested, excited, ready for anything. That would be high energy. We naturally associate the term "low energy" with sluggishness and lack of enthusiasm, and that's true to a degree. But in this case, it can also mean relaxed.

For instance, you may have a friend you can always talk to, who will listen calmly, without interrupting, and thinks about her responses. She makes you feel calm and confident. You know she's not "high energy," so in this case, she's low energy, but the good kind.

Now, plot your people. Starting with the first name on your list, use the blue pen for friends (for example). One by one, think about whether this friend makes you feel positive or negative (and how much), and if they transmit high energy or low energy. When you're trying to place someone, be conscious of your Red and Green Egos, and of the Mean Girls as well. Think about **why** you're putting someone to the left or right of the center. No wrong answers, just conscious ones. Do this with different colors for different groups, each person represented by a colorful dot (use names if you'd like, but we're looking for an overall impression, not one that's people-specific). You should end up with a view of how your relationships fall on the spectrum of high and low, positive and negative.

When you're finished, you may realize, "My friends are the best, a mix of high and calm energy, all of them positive. I need to appreciate them more!" or "I really want to set a goal for myself to focus on being more high energy and positive, and I'm going to do that with the people who make it easier for me." Regularly taking stock of your relationships and energy levels with this graph will allow you to be gently aware of who you're spending your time with and how it's affecting you. It's a beautifully eye-opening exercise and will help you visualize your orbit of relationships as well as the energy you're emitting and receiving.

# But wait...

# MAKE IT HAPPEN

Plot your relationships on this graph using different colors for family, friends, and colleagues. Begin identifying a pattern. For example, do some of your friends bring you down while most of your colleagues bring you up? Vice versa? Ask yourself how the energy you surround yourself with affects you day to day and month to month.

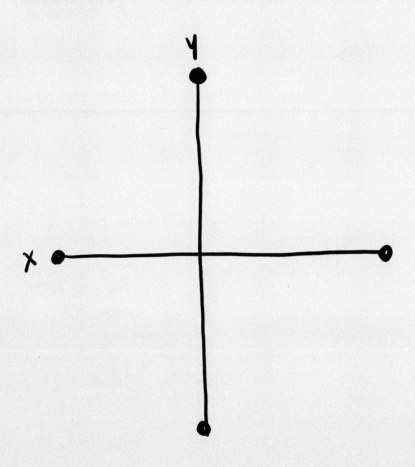

# ... there's more.

## EMOTIONAL FREQUENCY

Have you ever met someone who checks all the boxes, who you
*should* be best friends with, but you just don't "click"? For so long
I didn't have the language for this, and as a result I was very black-
and-white about all my relationships. Either we got along or we
didn't. If we didn't "click," that translated to "I don't like this
person" or "bad vibes." Over the years, as I've worked on building
communities, I've recognized that we need to pay close attention to
what I call "emotional frequency." A frequency is like a channel on
a TV or radio station. Every human tunes in to different channels
throughout their lives. Not everyone tunes in to the same channel at
the same time. As I'm writing this, I'm on a plane flying from New
York to LA, and I can see several screens; each seat with its own
personal TV. I'm marveling at how every single
screen has a different show, game, or movie
on it. Kids are watching cartoons, moms
are playing Candy Crush, teens are
watching ESPN, and dozens

of different movies are playing. Seeing all the diverse selections is a tangible reminder that everyone is tuned in to different frequencies. I like to picture everyone with a little antenna sticking out above their heads, tuning in to different channels. If we could see that we are all tuned to different channels, based on what's in our backpacks, we would feel more understood and would judge one another less negatively. These days when I don't click with someone, instead of going to a negative place, I can confidently say, "She's a nice person. Super energetic and friendly! We're just not on the same frequency!" **It's freeing.**

## The expression "You are as good as the five closest friends you keep" is real, y'all.

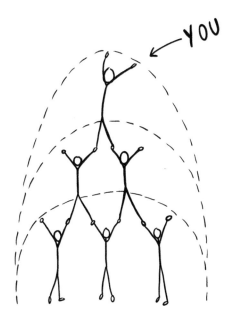

## REFRESH

Now imagine that at every moment of every day, you can choose to reset and refresh your energy and start from a neutral place at the center of the graph. Before we drift into the negative quadrants, we can actively make a choice at any moment to refresh and reset our energy. I say *refresh* because when I think of that word I think of a nice hot (or cold) shower and that "*ahhhh*" feeling I get from cleaning off the grime of the day and starting anew. Here's the thing: Refreshing doesn't just have to be physical; it can be energetic too. You can be angry in one moment and choose to reset and refresh. You can be sad and anxious in another moment and then make a conscious effort to refresh. You can feel lethargic and lazy and take a walk and refresh. You can get into arguments with friends or loved ones and ask, "Can we refresh?"

Let's remember: We are not bound to any energetic feeling. At any given moment, we can forgive, gently acknowledge, and give ourselves and others permission to refresh.

# MAKE IT HAPPEN

When you're feeling energetically disorganized—upset, anxious, angry, hurt, tired, depressed, scared—make a conscious effort to refresh. You have a choice. Ask yourself at any given moment, "Why is my energy here? Is this where I want to be? What's behind all of this? Can I gently acknowledge this energy and let it move through me?" Once you ask yourself these questions, you can reset your energy in any way that works. I like to find a doorway and just walk through it thinking "Energy reset!" the way we would say "Do over!" when we were kids.

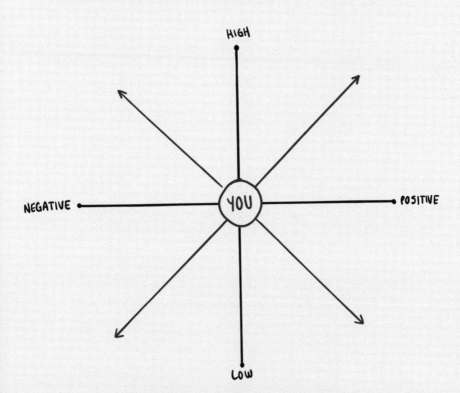

**ENERGY REFRESH PRACTICE**

# At any moment, you have a choice to refresh and reset your energy.

## How to Release Your D.O.S.E.

Understanding your brain chemistry is vital to understanding how to protect, reset, and increase your energy. There are four main brain chemicals responsible for your happiness and energy levels—Dopamine, Oxytocin, Serotonin, and Endorphins. When I discovered that the acronym for these happy brain chemicals spelled out the word *D.O.S.E.*, I almost fell out of my chair. I mean, right?! The dictionary defines *dose* as "a quantity of a medicine or drug taken or recommended to be taken at a particular time." But what if we learned to get our daily D.O.S.E. *naturally*? It would be a Star Wars Jedi kind of D.O.S.E., because it's our mind naturally showing us what we are capable of achieving without drugs or alcohol if we *just focus on it.*

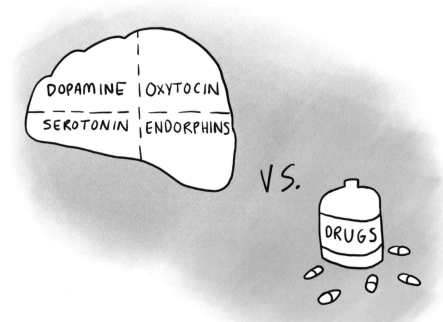

# D.O.S.E. CIRCUIT TRAINING

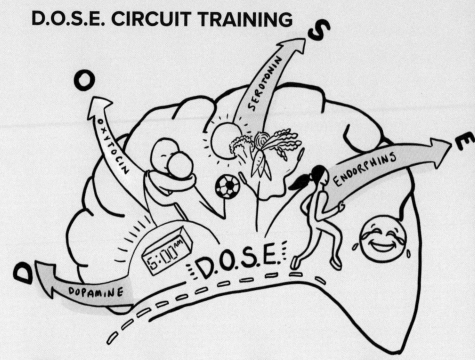

# D O S E

### DOPAMINE

Activated by pleasure and reward

Put your gym shoes on, listen to happy music, and go! Just the act of getting out the door will release dopamine. You're getting sh*t done!

### OXYTOCIN

Activated by physical touch

Make an effort to hug someone today instead of shaking their hand. Positive human touch releases oxytocin and it's vital for our health and happiness.

### SEROTONIN

Activated by mood, behavior, appetite, sleep

Increase your serotonin levels naturally: Go outside and get some sun! Work out or share three things you're grateful for when you wake up.

### ENDORPHINS

Activated by working out, getting heart rate up

Release your endorphins naturally: Exercise! Run! Dance! Burn calories! Laugh!

## WHY DO WE SEPARATE OUR BODIES FROM OUR MINDS?

We go to therapists for our minds and go to the gym for our bodies—forgetting that they're intertwined and connected. Why do we sit in chairs to talk about our feelings and exercise our bodies without understanding the effect on our minds?

To truly understand energy, we must first understand the interconnectivity between our bodies and our minds.

Sit with that for a moment. *Do you compartmentalize your mind and body?*

Now imagine if we could go to a ***Mind Gym.***

# What if this Mind Gym had fitness circuits for both our brains and our bodies?

We would quickly learn how to release our D.O.S.E. naturally in the same way we currently build our muscles and strengthen our cardio. Since I've been D.O.S.E.-ing for the last five years and focusing

on this natural release, I've felt the most epic highs of my life. Now when I'm out and friends ask me what I'm on, I smile and say, "I'm D.O.S.E.-ing." When they reply, "Dosing on what?!" I answer, "On myself!" And then I dance away.

# What D.O.S.E.-ing Actually Does to Our Brains

## Dopamine

Dopamine is a neurotransmitter that helps control your brain's reward and pleasure centers. It motivates you to take action toward your goals and gives you a rush of reinforcing pleasure when you achieve each goal. When I wake up and go to the gym (or to Daybreaker ☺), I get an exciting dopamine rush. It's my brain saying, "Good job, Radha! You set a goal for yourself and did it!" It's our brain high-fiving and congratulating us for getting sh*t done. Any goal we hit is rewarded by dopamine.

As with everything, there's a good side and a dark side to dopamine. The dark side is our addictive tendencies toward our phones and our brains tricking us into thinking, "That feels good!" It's the dings and notifications that lure us deeper into our phones, looking for the reward of a "like" or amusing tweet, and push us farther away from real connection. As I mentioned before, app developers have learned all the tricks from casinos! As you become more self-aware, you'll actually feel the pull of addiction to checking your phone. That's the first step to being able to resist! I'll keep on giving you suggestions on how to do that—and soon you'll find you'd rather check in with your body than your phone.

## Oxytocin

Oxytocin is often referred to as the "cuddle hormone." When we hug, touch, or kiss someone, our oxytocin levels increase. Social recognition, forming trust, reducing fear, and being generous are all by-products of oxytocin release. As psychotherapist Ranjan Patel beautifully said, "Biologically, we're born with the drive to touch. Psychologically, we thrive when touched, and spiritually, we grow with it. . . . Without touch, we would have no life on this planet, and without it, we would die as a species. Deep in our heart, we're hungry for it, and when we get it, we're jolted into pure sensate feeling."

Patel goes on to say, "In a famed study, a researcher studied how many times friends touched each other while sitting at a café. In Mexico City, couples touched each other 185 times. In Paris, 115 times. In London, zero times. In Gainesville, Florida, twice. We are not a touch-oriented culture. For all our obsession with sex, in contrast to other cultures, Americans are physically starved."

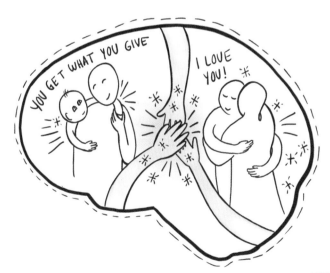

While building trust is a great by-product of an oxytocin release, there is an aspect of it that we should be aware of. **Oxytocin Overload** can make us feel territorial over our friendships and communities. From a macro level, Oxytocin Overload can also inspire cliques, groupthink, and ethnocentrism (where we think our culture or group is better or more important than others). I've definitely felt territorial when my best girlfriend started hanging out with another friend. At the time, I didn't have a language for that feeling. While I was happy that she had made another friend, I was also irrationally jealous about their new budding relationship. It was a feeling I had to face and overcome. Now I can tell when I'm getting territorial and I acknowledge the Oxytocin Overload and let that feeling move through me toward a more supportive place.

### Serotonin

Serotonin is considered a natural mood stabilizer and helps to reduce depression and regulate anxiety. It's also the brain chemical that helps with sleeping, eating, and digesting. We feel calmer, happier, and more focused when our levels are normal. When we feel significant or important, our serotonin flows. This is why belonging to a group or community feels so good—when we're a part of something bigger than ourselves, our serotonin levels increase. On the flip side, when we feel lonely or depressed, our serotonin is low. Here are ways to increase your serotonin levels naturally:

Go outside and get some sun!

Work out!

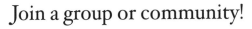

Practice gratitude and take a moment to reflect on past achievements!

Join a group or community!

The thing is, when humans were hunters and gatherers, we would spend all day outside running around in the sun getting exercise and lots of light. Now that we're more sedentary and indoors most of the day, it's harder to get our serotonin release, and many of us turn to pills or unnatural means to lift our mood. So when you're feeling down, ask yourself if you've been outside or practiced gratitude or connected with like-minded friends and see where that takes you!

### Endorphins

Endorphins are morphine-like chemicals released from the pituitary gland that help diminish pain and trigger positive feelings. They get released in times of stress, pain, orgasm, and strenuous exercise. The terms "second wind" and "runner's high" come from that endorphin release. Here are a few ways to release your endorphins naturally:

## Exercise! Run! Dance! Burn calories! Laugh! Listen to comedy! Learn a few jokes! Build your sense of humor!

Now, instead of thinking, "I have to go to the gym and work out," I think, "I have to go to the gym and release my D.O.S.E.," which gets me excited to put on my gym shoes!

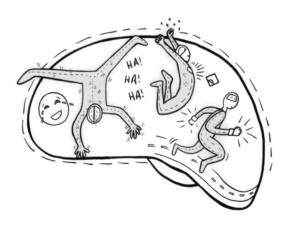

# Your Daily D.O.S.E.

**D** **DOPAMINE:**
Get sh*t done!
Show up.

**O** **OXYTOCIN:**
Give five hugs today!

**S** **SEROTONIN:**
Go outside for
twenty minutes!

**E** **ENDORPHINS:**
Get your heart rate up!
Sweat! Dance! Laugh!

# Use the doorway trick to refresh your energy.

D.O.S.E.-ing also helps you hold your temperature and maintain a positive energy. I love the expression "Be the thermostat, not the thermometer." It means be the type of person that holds your temperature at a sunny 70 degrees, like a thermostat, regardless of the energy around you, rather than being a thermometer and mirroring others' energy.

I have a trick that reminds me to be the thermostat: I use a doorway as my energy-refreshing opportunity. Before I enter any room, I like to stop at the door, take a few deep breaths, and remind myself to "be the thermostat and not the thermometer." If I have a stressful conversation, going through the doorway reminds me that I can refresh at any time and choose a new, energetic direction. It actually works—try it!

## FOCUS ON FIVE SENSE FRIENDS (FSFs)

We have five incredible senses, but use only one or two in our texting and phone interactions. What's up with that?! We've replaced our ability to "feel" one another through our animal instincts and five senses with "judging our emoji game." When all five of our senses are activated and firing on all cylinders, we feel happiest and most connected to one another.

Let's focus on cultivating Five

# MAKE IT HAPPEN

This week, anytime you go through a doorway, take a deep breath, allow yourself to refresh your energy, and think:

BE THE THERMOSTAT

(NOT THE THERMOMETER)

Sense Friends—or FSFs. I've made a rule for myself: For every friend I keep in touch with primarily electronically, I have to cultivate one FSF who I will see regularly and engage with fully. Let's stop replacing FSFs with Instagram followers! Followers are for marketing ourselves, FSFs are for feeding our souls and experiencing an authentic relationship. Let's also keep from confusing the use and enjoyment of all our senses with being sexual. That's great, but there's more to it! Paying attention to our five senses in *all* our relationships, not just our romantic ones, is vitally important in developing a sense of belonging.

## So What Would Your World Look Like If You Focused on Being an FSF?

**SEEING:** Making eye contact is the backbone of belonging and connection.

**HEARING:** Listening to one another allows for love and empathy to grow.

**TASTING:** Eat together! Feed each other! It has been a crucial part of connection since the beginning of time.

**TOUCHING:** We cannot survive without touch and skin to skin connection. Hugging, holding hands, or cuddle-puddling is key to feeling a sense of belonging.

**SMELLING:** We are all animals, and getting used to one another's smells inspires a sense of belonging—our pheromones dancing together allow for a deeper connection.

# MAKE IT HAPPEN

Close your eyes and activate each of your senses (yes, even sight!). Touch your arm, taste what's on your tongue right now, smell the room you're in, and listen for any sounds. What do you hear? What do you smell? What do you taste? What texture do you feel? What do you see when your eyes are closed? This sensory awareness is going to be important for when we Go OUT.

## BE AN FYF—F*CK YEAH! FRIEND

If there's one thing you get out of this book, this is it.

At a dinner party, I asked my dear friend Mark what his New Year's resolution was. He said, "I'm going to be a f*ck yeah friend this year. I've been so focused on work; but this year, I want to enthusiastically say yes to all social engagements with humans I want to connect with more meaningfully." As I thought about it, I realized being an FYF (F*ck Yeah! Friend) is the cornerstone of making friends and building community. My happiness and success as a community builder are directly attributable to being an FYF and surrounding myself with other FYFs. Being an FYF means your body language says, "F*CK YEAH! I'M IN." It means not being too cool for school and not shoulder-shrugging. Being an FYF means you SHOW UP.

# Fully. Presently. Lovingly. Energetically. Empathetically. Intentionally. Courageously. Vulnerably. Curiously.

Also, saying no to misaligned or depleting communities will give you the space to be an FYF for those who inspire a real sense of belonging and will fill up your tank. Developing your filter by simply being aware of who you're saying yes and no to will be game changing as you Go OUT.

# MAKE IT HAPPEN

Notice how you're showing up this week. What are you saying yes and no to? Are you leaning in and saying an enthusiastic YES!!? Or are you putting on a mask of "cool" or "I don't care"? Get gently curious as to why you're acting that way. Try being an FYF this week and see what happens. What happens when you FULLY show up? See how it impacts your day! "Be an FYF!" is now in many employee handbooks too! #proud

# Showing Up

SHOWING UP is key to making real friends and building lasting communities. We've made phrases like "I'm overwhelmed," "It's so intense," and "It's so hard and scary" a part of our day-to-day language. That way of being gives us support and excuses that keep us from putting our shoes on and showing up. You end up cheating yourself—and others.

SHOWING UP is more than physical. You're not showing up if you're distracted, on your phone, inauthentic, or in the clouds. Showing up means helping out. Showing up means adding value. Showing up means wagging your tail. It's also about being CONSISTENT and patient. Belonging develops over time, and it rewards you forever.

SIT WITH THIS. And then go back through Part 1 as often as you can. These ideas can serve you all your life, through different ages, stages, and the inevitable ups and downs we all experience. When you show up, you are not alone. So keep Going In to always, eventually, Go Out!

# GOING OUT

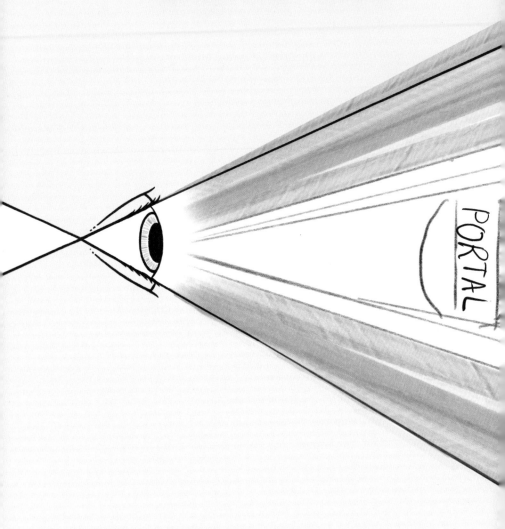

PORTAL

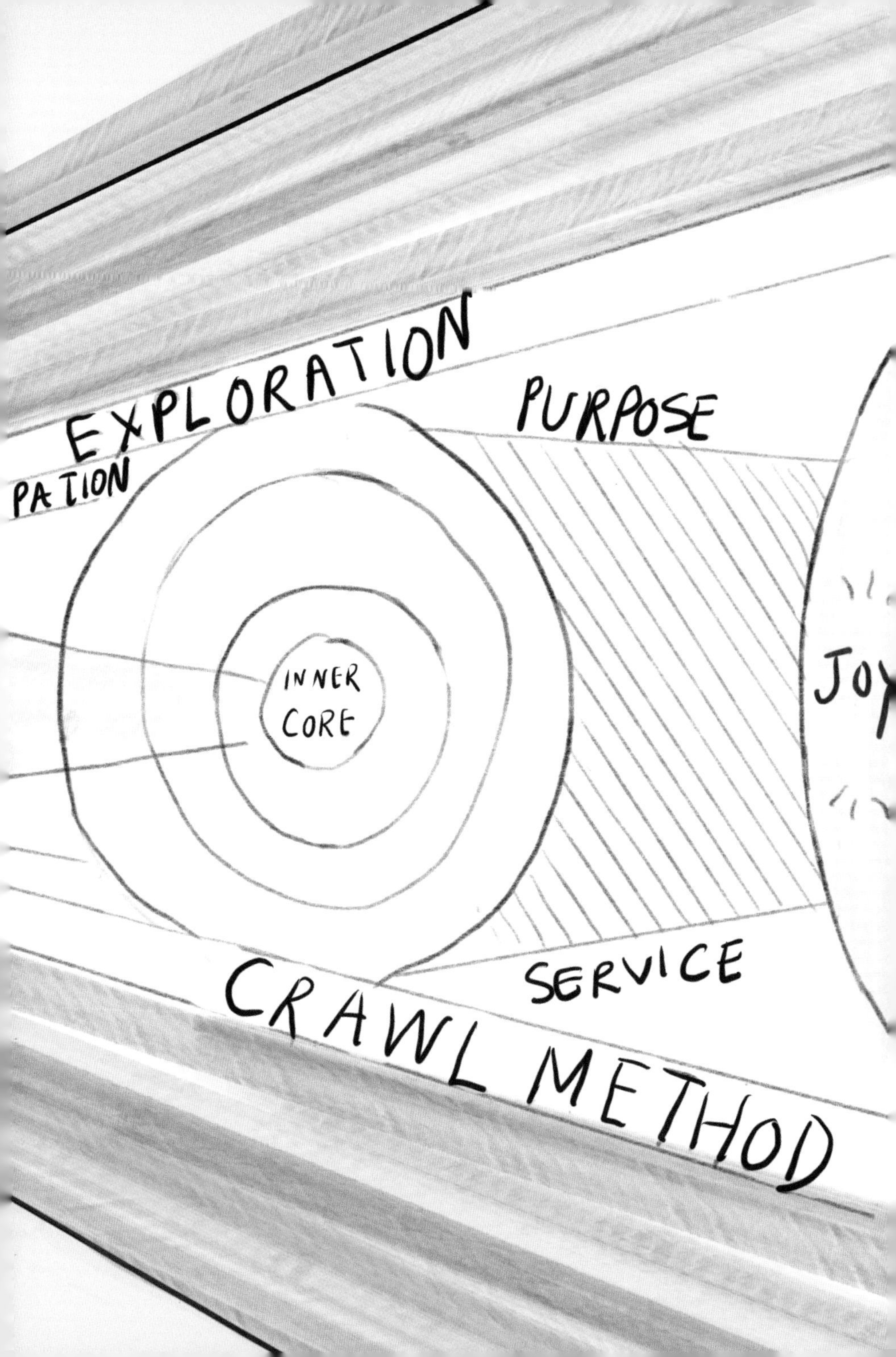
EXPLORATION
PATION
PURPOSE
INNER
CORE
JOY
SERVICE
CRAWL METHOD

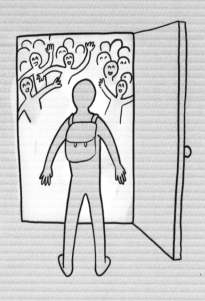

This is where life gets
really exciting.
Buckle your seatbelt—
we're Going OUT.

# CHAPTER 5

# Where to Find Your People

## The Four Stages of Community

When you move to a new city, start school or a new job, or just realize you want new relationships in your life—where do you look? It can be overwhelming. Understanding the Four Stages of Community will help you navigate this expansive and often paralyzing world and give you clear steps to answer the question, "Where the heck do I find my people?!"

# Four Stages of Community

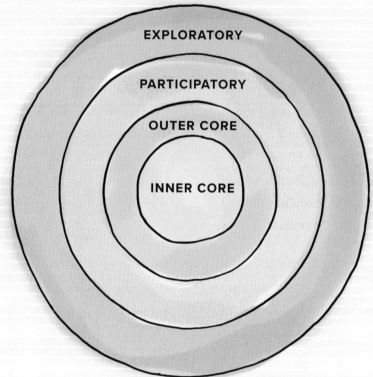

EXPLORATORY

PARTICIPATORY

OUTER CORE

INNER CORE

To find your people, you
have to be willing—and
generous—with your energy.

© 2017 RADHA AGRAWAL

## STAGE 1: EXPLORATORY

It is easy and tempting to fall into communities or groups that are convenient. Who doesn't want easy and convenient? But convenience doesn't always lead to best. When we do a full Mars Rover exploration of what's around us, we're more likely to end up in communities that are soul-filling. Think of this as a period of learning about yourself. What are you excited about right now? What are you reading? Consuming? Creating? What do you want to contribute to a community? Go into every situation curious, with your beginner's mind open.

Flip back to Chapter 3 and do a refresher on your Values, Interests, and Abilities (VIA), then start mapping out your city (or state or town or wherever) for places and groups that align with your interests. **Exploration can also start online.** This is where the internet is magic! Just don't get stuck there. It's meant to be a stepping-stone to get offline and interact with real humans. As you explore, connect with the curious animal inside of you that says, "What's out there?!" It may take a leap of faith if you think of yourself as shy or a homebody, or you think you've seen it all already, but curiosity and exploration are what brought humankind to where we are today and make life way more fun! Do it your way—maybe quietly at first—

but do it!

what are you consuming?

What's there?

what are you excited about?

what are you reading?

what are you creating?

You can start with smaller meet-up groups or dinner events, where it's more intimate and you'll have a chance to engage right away, or larger groups like festivals and community events, where you're anonymous and just checking things out. Either way, the idea is that it's low-risk and low-stress.

Here are some things that worked for me when I found myself in a new city where I didn't know anyone:

• Reaching out via Facebook to specific friends and acquaintances who I knew shared my values and interests (while avoiding the endless scroll) and asking if they could connect me with like-minded communities.

• Joining FB groups in that city and going to meetup.com, where I found communities that matched my interests, and showing up to the meetups that had at least twenty people attending the event.

• Going to the local yoga studio for drop-in classes.

• In various cities, I have joined a soccer league, softball league, dodgeball league, and kickball league.

• My twin sister, Miki, and I played soccer in college, so when we moved to New York City, we went to Central Park and jumped in a pickup soccer game. We made our first friends on the dirt fields by Sheep Meadow.

• We also joined a choir in Brooklyn and were the youngest by about thirty years. After twelve weeks of rehearsals we sang with the Brooklyn Symphony Orchestra!

It may take you three weeks or three months to figure out what you're actually interested in, so don't rush this process. It's the most important step, as it will lead you to your *Inner Core Community*. Stay patient and keep going back to your Values, Interests, and Abilities, and stay authentic and true to what lights your fire. Don't just do what everyone else is doing, but stay open to opportunities that feel like a stretch for you. There will be humans who love the same things you do and who will inspire you in ways you can't imagine! Go in with a positive attitude, but since you're just exploring, you don't have anything to lose and don't have to be gung ho about something before you know if it's for you. You really need only the amount of energy it takes to get yourself out the door. **Showing up** is the goal at this stage of the process, and everything stems from there.

# MAKE IT HAPPEN

Find five to ten communities and groups that interest you (meetup.com and/or Facebook are good places to start), then join the groups and start showing up! Explore at least one new group that aligns with your Values, Interests, and Abilities this week. Plan to get through one group a week for the next five to ten weeks. Think about anything positive that interests you right now. If you don't think you have any interests, dig deep—you really do. Just put on your shoes and show up.

SHOW UP

# STAGE 2: PARTICIPATORY

Once you've explored five to ten communities, narrow them down into two or three groups and start participating in making them better or volunteering your time. This is where your FYF attitude comes into play.

Participation with a positive attitude is the ultimate key to belonging. You'll feel the most emotionally invested and connected to others in the group by getting your hands dirty and offering your time and energy to enhance the community experience. The sweat and effort of doing something for the benefit of the greater whole will fill you with the most satisfaction and joy. This is also how people come to view you as someone they want to be around, know more about, and care for. **These are the cornerstones of belonging: being an FYF and participation.**

### Participation at Home

"Home" feels like home because we put so much effort into building our bookshelves, cooking our meals, making our bed, cleaning our bathroom, and doing our laundry. We are emotionally invested in spaces and communities when we wholeheartedly participate in creating and nurturing them. When we do chores around the house, it makes us feel more connected to our family and household. So let's reframe "annoying chores" for "participation and belonging"!

# Participation at the Office

When Eli started working at his first job out of
college, he created a fun Friday afternoon activity
to bring the office together. For a simple game that
needed only the conference room, he created charts
with everyone's name and had tournament-style
rounds where his coworkers competed against one
another, with made-up prizes for the weekly winners.
From there, he organized the office soccer team,
lacrosse team, and poker night, and even had custom
shorts and jerseys made. He included everyone in his
office, from his sixty-year-old bosses and managers to
entry-level twenty-year-olds. It created a strong office
culture and community, and everyone who participated
felt more connected to the office and team. The great
thing is that you don't have to be the one creating and
organizing if that's not your thing. Just participate
with an FYF attitude. When everyone participates,
bonds strengthen.

Organized religions, the military, sports teams,
and political and philanthropic organizations have
figured this out and inspire participation through
service and ritual. This creates deep loyalty and
connection among their members. To feel connected to
anything in life, participation is KEY.

**STAGGERING STAT:** Alex Sheen, founder of *Because I said I would*—a nonprofit focused on accountability and keeping one's word—discovered that 75 percent of Americans did not volunteer a SINGLE HOUR to a nonprofit or civic organization in 2016. While we spend millions of collective hours on the internet each week, three out of four Americans have not made any time for community service or volunteerism in their lives. What would the world look like if every human participated in one day of service per year?

7.5 billion adults
× 8 hours in one day of service
_____

60 billion hours of community service per year

It would make a difference, don't you think? So let's take a day off from our internet participation and offer it to the world instead!

### Simple Ways to Participate in Making Your Community Better

Here are a few simple examples of ways our friends contribute and participate in our community and add value to our collective experience. See if any of these sound like you. If not, refer back to Chapter 3, look at your Interests and Abilities, and start thinking of ways you can participate and contribute! If everyone took the time to do something, imagine how much more fun and meaningful life would be!

- **MAKE A PLAYLIST AND SHARE IT WITH FRIENDS**—
My brother-in-law Andrew makes amazing
monthly playlists for our community and shares
them for everyone's enjoyment. He spends hours
every month creating these playlists. He loves discovering new
music, so it's equally fun for him to create them!

- **ASK THOUGHTFUL QUESTIONS**—Andrew is also known for his
question-asking game. He has specially tailored questions that get
right into your backpack. And he's just as good at listening!

- **BRING INSTRUMENTS**—Matisse and Vic bring instruments to
most gatherings they show up to. They'll do a full-out
performance, or just provide a little accompaniment to
bring up the mood and share their instruments with
friends.

- **ENHANCE THE AMBIANCE OF A ROOM**—Brooke loves to add
candles, blankets, and incense to make any room where she's hosting
friends more cozy. She also dims the lighting to create a more
inviting atmosphere.

- **MASSAGE**—Elliott has magic hands and will massage
friends' backs and hands (in a nonsexual way!). He gives
amazing hugs and really contributes friendly energy to
any room he's in.

- **COOK A MEAL AND INVITE PEOPLE OVER FOR DINNER TO GET TO KNOW THEM BETTER**—Eli and Lilly are master chefs and will spend hours cooking delicious meals for our community. In turn, our friends support their efforts by helping to serve, clean, and do the dishes.

- **GIVE THE COMMUNITY SOMETHING IT NEEDS**—Gio loves music and is passionate about getting his community together to dance and connect. He loves a party with a good speaker system, but since they're expensive to rent, he built speakers from scratch and keeps them available for his Washington, DC, community to borrow free of charge. The community supports him in maintaining the equipment by giving small donations whenever they can.

- **ENROLL IN A CONFERENCE ON A TOPIC THAT INTERESTS YOU**—Years ago, Miki told me about a conference called Summit Series where thousands of young, curious entrepreneurs gather. I went the following year and made many of my closest, longest-lasting friends.

- **VOLUNTEER FOR A COMMUNITY ORGANIZATION**—Catherine Hoke started an organization called Defy Ventures that takes incarcerated men, women, and youth, and transforms their hustle by mentoring and teaching them entrepreneurial skills. Anyone can volunteer! #inspired

# MAKE IT HAPPEN

Participate in one thing outside of your normal routine for the next four weeks. Narrow down the list of things you explored in your Exploratory Stage to activities and communities that you loved—or think you could love. Get your hands dirty and SHOW UP! See how it feels to get physically involved in something! Have the courage to participate in whatever piques your curiosity. Think about bringing something relevant and enjoyable to share—music and food are often appreciated. Check in with your VIA chart and contribute!

## List three to five ways in which you can participate and contribute to the communities you're interested in.

# STAGES 3 AND 4:
# OUTER CORE AND INNER CORE

## This is where the magic happens.

At this point in your Four Stages of Community, you've gotten intentional, explored, participated, given energy, and shown up. You know when you meet a new friend who fills up your Energy Tank and who provides an *Equal Energy Exchange.* You feel that exhale of "I'm home." This is someone who embodies the qualities you wrote down in Chapter 3. Their energy really matches your energy. You're genuinely curious about them and feel their authentic curiosity about you. Your values are aligned, your interests are aligned, and you feel truly "seen" for your entire colorful rainbow. These are the relationships to really invest in and spend time showing up for. And chances are, they have a few friends who are like you too and can be your portal to amazing Outer Core and Inner Core Communities. **Energy is your essential guide to belonging. You have to protect it but also be generous with it if you want to find real happiness and community.**

You can't feel that exhale of "I'm home" if someone lives on the left side of the Axis of Energy or if you're on different frequencies. I have an *80/20 Rule*. If 80 percent of the time I feel that exhale of "I'm home" and 20 percent of the time we're on different frequencies, the friendship is worth continuing to invest in. When I'm on different frequencies or arguing more often than not, I have an honest conversation with myself about whether this friendship or relationship is still feeding me.

I've separated your Outer Core and Inner Core Communities into two stages because Outer Core encompasses the larger group of friends or community (fifty to one hundred community members) whose values and interests are similar to yours, and Inner Core

represents the three to ten friends who are the closest and make you feel the most secure. I informally polled hundreds of community members and discovered that everyone had at least three and at most ten Inner Core Community members they felt significantly connected to at any given time. Think about what number would make *you* happy. British anthropologist Robin Dunbar proposed that humans can comfortably maintain 150 stable relationships (Outer Core) and go deep with five friends (Inner Core).

The lines between Outer Core and Inner Core can become blurred as we move between cities and jobs. Almost fifty-five million Americans are freelancers—35 percent of our workforce—and that number is only going up.* We grow closer to the friends we have access to—which changes often in many people's lives as they change jobs and addresses.

Getting to this stage of connection may take six months to a year. Maybe more. Online connections don't count! Don't get discouraged! It's *supposed* to take time to go through the stages. Reframe your feelings from "Why is it taking so long to find my people?" to "They're out there waiting to be found so I'll keep going to spaces and places that pique my curiosity!"

*Upwork and the Freelancers Union, "Freelancing in America: 2016," https://www.upwork.com/i/freelancing-in-america/2016.

# The Inner and the Outer Core

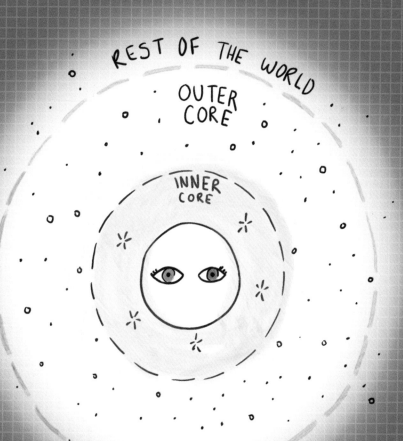

REST OF THE WORLD

OUTER CORE

INNER CORE

The longer it takes, the more intentional you will get, the more you will cherish those friendships, and the more you will learn about yourself in the process. It may happen quickly too! Just keep getting *Vulnerable, Intentional, and Courageous.* I call it "getting VIC"—it's **victorious to be able to access our powerful human traits and gently notice when we are wearing our protective masks.**

Whenever we interview our *Community Catalysts* (the Local Lead Producers) for Daybreaker, we do a full exploration of the city we're in and interview dozens of candidates before making a decision. We then fly them to New York City and invite them to participate in creating a Daybreaker with us to get to know them better. We can discern pretty quickly if this is someone with whom we feel an Equal Energy Exchange. We look for whether they hang out with their Red or Green Egos and Mean Girls or Soul Sisters. When we feel that exhale of "I'm home" with that person, we get excited because we know they will likely be our Portal to a like-minded community in their city.

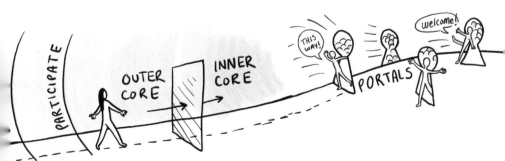

## LET'S GET INTO PORTALS!

A Portal is your gate-
way to an authentic community
that shares your values and interests.
Portals are found offline and are often the
influencer's influencer. A Portal is a human you
*actually meet* and connect with in your Exploratory
and Participatory Stages who can help you find
your Outer and Inner Core Communities. This is
a magical human with whom you feel an Equal
Energy Exchange and with whom time stands
still. Portals are generous, they love to
connect people, and they operate
with little fear or insecurity. They help you
find more like-minded
people who are aligned
with your VIA. Portals introduce you to other humans who
make you think, "Wow! Where have
you been all my life?" They are also
thoughtful about who they bring into the
community. They help to monitor the energy
and make sure everyone fits and feels good.

## GETTING TO KNOW A PORTAL

**PORTALS ARE FIVE SENSE FRIENDS (FSFs)** and are not just found online or on social media. You *can* explore online, but have to show up in person to connect with your Portal.

**"I'VE BEEN TEXTING AND CALLING MY PORTAL WITH NO RESPONSE!** When do I know to keep pushing or to back down and move on?" Remember, Portals are busy and already have a community they're tending to—you're the new kid on the block. Don't take it personally! Rather than just asking to meet for coffee or "pick their brain" (ouch that hurts!), offer to support them by volunteering your time—help cook a meal or take the trash out. Get creative with how you can connect with your Portal. Keep following up courageously and vulnerably if you truly felt an Equal Energy Exchange. Remember, energy has to be felt on both sides!

## MAKE IT HAPPEN

Follow up with your Portal this week! Or go deep with one person this week with whom you feel an Equal Energy Exchange, and who's not family or someone you're dating. Get Vulnerable, Intentional, and Courageous and keep following up and offering support!

**ABOUT CLOSE FRIENDS:** We often silo our close relationships into different buckets—"this is my workout friend, this is my college friend, this is my party friend, this is my Harry Potter friend"—to protect ourselves, or because it's just easier. The old paradigm was "Don't introduce people to one another. They'll leave you behind. Protect yourself!" or "What if they all start hanging out without me?" or "It's just easier to have different friends for different interests. . . . " I felt that in my twenties, and it was exhausting to juggle all these friendships that ultimately weren't even feeding me. While it was sometimes fun to run around and I always had stories to tell, I didn't feel a real commitment to anyone, which in the end made me feel empty.

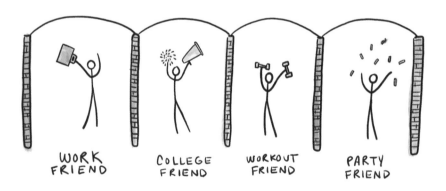

WORK FRIEND    COLLEGE FRIEND    WORKOUT FRIEND    PARTY FRIEND

# When I started over at thirty, I was intentional about finding friends who I could do it all with and who could love one another as a collective.

Rather than being scared about connecting others, I was excited to try it without fear and with an open heart. There would be no competition and no juggling friend groups, and the rule was no shit-talking or sneaking around behind one another's backs. We would all be respectful of one another and honor each other. Honesty, inclusivity, and transparency were our core tenets. If we had a problem, we would talk to the person we had a problem with, not someone else.

And wow, *what a difference it made*.

It took faith, as well as getting vulnerable, intentional, and courageous, but I gave it a shot, and my life became exponentially richer and more open. **As I introduced people to one another, they introduced me to their people, and we created a culture of connection rather than of separation.**

That said, my friend Cordelia shared that she excitedly introduced two friends who hit it off, but when she asked one of the friends a few weeks later what she was doing that night, her friend lied about hanging out with the other friend, which hurt Cordelia's feelings when she later found out. Had her friend just said, "I'm hanging out with your friend and getting to know her better!

Thank you for the intro!" that would have been great and Cordelia would have been thrilled! But it was the omission of the truth that was unnecessary. While Cordelia's friends probably just wanted to avoid an awkward moment, it wasn't the respectful or kind approach. Again, honesty, inclusivity, and transparency are the keys here.

It took me many years to realize that I didn't feel like myself in my twenties because I fell into friendships and relationships that made me feel insecure, and I allowed myself to spend time with people who hung out on the left side of the Axis of Energy, with their Red Egos and Mean Girls, more often than not. Until I turned thirty, I was swept up in "the scene" and never once stopped to do a deep dive into what *I* wanted out of this magical life. When I focused on radiating my authentic energy, being generous by making introductions, connecting people, and showing up with an FYF attitude, everything changed. Sometimes (OK, most of the time), we get in our own dang way.

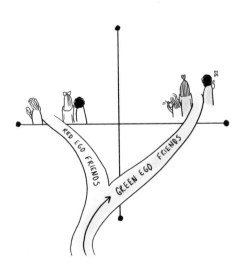

I was talking with a fellow Community Architect living in Chattanooga recently over brunch. Sheldon and I got deep into the topic of Inner Core Community. He looked at me with earnest eyes and said, "For the last three years, I've been so busy building communities for everyone else. I realized that I didn't have my own Inner Core Community and I had positioned myself on the outside of the communities I was helping to build." When he realized this and began focusing on deepening *his* relationships, his whole life changed. After much persuasion, he went to a men's retreat and met five amazing guys who were also starved for meaningful connection. "It definitely wasn't an overnight thing. I had already met all those guys before the retreat. The retreat was where I felt compelled to begin spending more time investing seriously in those relationships. We meet every week now—a 5:30 a.m. meet-up every other Friday and 8 p.m. at a local brewery every other Wednesday. I knew that my heart longed for deeper, more meaningful fellowship with other guys, but I lacked the resolve and commitment to do what it takes to build those relationships. It's really easy to make excuses—even valid ones!— about why you shouldn't invest the time and energy. In my case these were things like: I need to spend more time with my family, I'm tired, I need to get to work early or stay late, I'd rather relax and watch Netflix, etc. The retreat created the space and time for me to reflect upon my life and consider the things I should be prioritizing.

When I started prioritizing these friendships, my relationship with my wife and three kids changed overnight. My relationship with my employees and business partners changed. As soon as I began investing in my personal relationships—making a commitment to see my group of friends once a week and going deeper with each of them—I became exponentially happier and I saw the power of what I was actually building."

It was yet another reminder that even the best Community Architects still need help addressing their own sense of belonging. He is definitely not alone!

You'll be going back to the Four Stages of Community all your life as you move places, change careers, and evolve as a human. You'll also be going through the Four Stages for your business, organization, or new job. Spend *real* time cultivating your Outer and Inner Core relationships and truly make an effort to meet regularly, even if life gets busy. Every year, reassess your Outer and Inner Core Communities and ask yourself if these relationships are feeding you. Write your friends' names down and get really honest with yourself as to how you're showing up for them and how they're showing up for you. I do this every year on my birthday. It's been wonderfully eye-opening and cathartic. The years that I didn't focus on relationships I was less happy (and healthy) and the years that I started getting intentional about them, my happiness and health were noticeably different. It's not a coincidence.

# Pro Tip:

When you hang out with an Outer or Inner Core Community member, before you say good-bye, schedule your next hang so you have something to look forward to. Be proactive about picking the next date together, on the spot! If you have to reschedule, that's fine, but at least it's on the calendar!

## STARTER KIT: COMMUNITY-BUILDING EVENT

If you want to be proactive and create an event that can help get you started on your journey to your Outer and Inner Core Communities, here are some tips.

I'll start with a story.

When my friend Tobias moved to San Francisco, he knew one person. He was feeling lonely and wanted to cultivate new friendships in the city around topics that he was passionate about.

Instead of sitting around or trolling bars, he decided to start a biweekly meet-up called "Good Drinks." He sat down, thought about the kinds of friends he wanted to make, and got intentional about meeting people who shared his interests in philanthropy and social impact. Then he created a simple Facebook event page called "Good Drinks," set a date for the first meeting, and wrote a short description about the idea behind the gathering. Over the next couple of weeks, he invited anyone who expressed any interest and who he thought could be a good fit. He posted to social media, asking friends in other cities to connect him to their friends in San Francisco, and then invited

those friends of friends by simply saying, "This is going to be fun! We have free drinks! Join us!" He spent forty dollars on drinks and arranged to hold the event at his office.

Leading up to the event he was nervous that no one would show up, but then he realized, "What do I have to lose? Worst case scenario, I hang out at my office for a few extra hours that day and have extra booze to try again in a few weeks."

To his excitement, five people showed up to his first event, which by his measure was a massive success! They had drinks and great conversations about current events, and everyone got along. When there was a lull in conversation, Tobias brought the whole party together by asking a few questions that he had prepared to keep the flow going. And it worked! For twelve months, he hosted "Good Drinks" every few weeks, and after a year he had hosted over two hundred people, seven of whom have become lifelong friends. All he needed was intention and courage to take the first step!

# The Six-Step Community Event Starter Kit

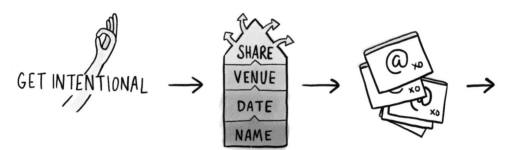

GET INTENTIONAL → SHARE VENUE DATE NAME → @ xo xo xo →

1. GET INTENTIONAL—What are you interested in and curious about? This is the most important thing to focus on!

2. GIVE YOUR EVENT A FUN NAME, set a date, find a venue, and create a Facebook event—or use your own method for spreading the word and getting responses.

3. START SENDING EMAILS to all of your contacts and ask them if they know anyone who fits your criteria, then post to your social media or on meetup.com. Be thoughtful about how you present the event. Would *you* want to attend it based on the description?

4. SPEND whatever you can afford on drinks and food. Or if your event is more action-oriented, make it easy for people to participate and have fun. If necessary, have a rain date and keep your guests informed if you're going to employ it.

5. PREPARE TWO TO THREE QUESTIONS to ask in case there's a lull in conversation. Also, when you get above ten people, it can be harder to bring everyone together into one single conversation, so questions can become icebreakers for two people to connect over instead.

6. CONSIDER A BIMONTHLY OR MONTHLY MEET-UP and stick with it! Community is built on accountability and consistently showing up!

Movements are built with deep intention and patience.

# CHAPTER 6

# The CRAWL Method

## How to Build Your Dream Community from Scratch

O nce you're comfortably established with your personal community, bring your discoveries into the world! Whether you're looking to organize larger events with more people or scale your community for your business or organization, the methods I outline here will get you there.

PATH TO COMMUNITY

# CRAWL is an acronym:

**C**  **CORE VALUES + CONSTRAINTS + CORE COMMUNITY**
Create the philosophical foundation for your community.

**R**  **RITUALS**
How rituals and participation are vital for inspiring loyalty and belonging.

**A**  **AESTHETICS**
Why aesthetics make or break community.

**W**  **WHY + WHAT**
Five must-answer questions before creating community.

**L**  **LANGUAGE**
The face of your community. Learn the difference between words and language.

Over the last several years, I've synthesized all my key insights from building communities in twenty-five cities and a dozen college campuses across the world and from countless conversations and workshops with other top Community Architects into the **CRAWL** method. It has been an essential guide to building our Daybreaker community around the globe.

Community takes time to build. You have to *crawl* before you run. So take your time, explore, get intentional, and be patient throughout this process. It's a marathon, not a sprint.

## DEFINE YOUR CORE VALUES, CONSTRAINTS, AND CORE COMMUNITY

The three Cs in the CRAWL method will help you create a solid foundation for your community.

Before you even think about your Community's Core Values, start by defining your *Personal* Core Values.

Go back to Chapter 3 and look at the values you added to your VIA circles. Now whittle down your values to three to five Core Values. A Core Value again is a non-negotiable and an umbrella that your interests and abilities can fit under. While they may change throughout your life, take some time to think about what you really value *today*. It can be as simple as concepts such as health, having fun, music, dancing, meditation, yoga, traveling, experiencing love, learning new things, running, or family. If you're still figuring out what *you* care about, you're not ready to start your own community just yet. Spend some more time Going IN.

I whittled down my values into three Personal Core Values that I could stay excited about for a very long time: *wellness, community,* and *fun*. I knew that if those three elements were involved, I could be on board with just about anything. With these Personal Core Values identified, I could now think about what kind of community I wanted to create and get really excited about.

## Simple Steps to Define Your Personal Core Values

**1.** Take some time to list ten values that deeply resonate with *you*. Look at your Values, Interests, and Abilities chart from Chapter 3. You can also Google "values" if you want some ideas, but don't let the internet sway your thoughts. Think about when you are happiest and most "in flow," or situations or events that light you up and that you reflect on for days. What was it about those moments that made the difference to you?

EMPATHY
HUMOR
QUALITY
STYLE
INNOVATION

CREATIVITY
HEALTH
EQUALITY
COMMUNICATION
EDUCATION

**2.** Now whittle your list down to three to five strong Core Values. What are your non-negotiables? For example, physical health, nutrition, and sleep are non-negotiables for me—when I stay on top of them, I feel like my truest self; when I don't, I feel unpredictable and out of sorts. As such, "wellness" is an easy Personal Core Value for me to identify. My friend Matisse loves learning about how our brain functions, so she's always reading books about it, posting on social media, and learning new techniques to relax our minds through meditation and music. Her Personal Core Values are mindfulness, learning, and creative expression.

**3.** Think about how you embody and/or model your Core Values. Are these values aspirational (are you reaching toward them?) or are they reflections (you already embody them)? Think about what feels natural to you, what doesn't feel like work, and what you love to talk about. And think about what values you *want* to embody but may not be quite there yet. This will give you clues about your own Personal Core Values.

# Once you've identified your Personal Core Values, then do the same for your dream community.

Identify five to ten Core Values that you'd like your community to embody. How do these Core Values align with what you'd like the community's purpose to be? What would you like to be sure are the community's non-negotiables?

When Matt and I launched Daybreaker, we knew we wanted it to be intentional and not just your typical "dance party." We were changing every aspect of the nightlife experience and our values had to reflect that—our events were in the morning, sober, and on weekdays before work! We were marrying the worlds of fitness and festival culture and were creating something completely new in two exciting and fast-growing spaces. So we spent several days going back and forth until we finally landed on our five Core Values. For every decision we would make going forward—from partners and performers to DJs we collaborated with to the food and beverages we would provide at our events—we'd look through the lens of these five Core Values:

 **WELLNESS:** Sweat, eat, and drink with intention. Be healthy inside and out.

 **CAMARADERIE:** Open your heart and connect with people. Find friends on the dance floor and outside of our events. Make your city feel like a village.

**SELF-EXPRESSION:** Be your gloriously unabashed self. Dance with reckless abandon, wear crazy costumes, let your freak flag fly!

 **MINDFULNESS:** Be here now. Put your phones away and be present in the moment. Revel in gratitude.

 **MISCHIEF:** Live life with a wink and push your boundaries. Play more!

These five Core Values would become the North Star for our community across the world. It's actually more fun (and freeing!) to create *within* a framework. It helps us know when to say yes and when to say no!

**DEFINE THE CONSTRAINTS THAT WILL SHAPE YOUR COMMUNITY.** Constraints are filters that give your community guardrails that help people decide if they want to join. They differ from Core Values, which are qualities that your community strives to live by.

For example, two Constraints for Louis Vuitton are "price" and "heritage," since their handbags are pricey and not everyone can afford them, and they're a heritage brand—meaning they keep to a traditional design—so those who like more modern designs may not be into their bags. Conversely, Louis Vuitton's Core Values are "innovative" and "creative," which are their guiding principles and totally different from their Constraints.

## AT DAYBREAKER, WE HAVE THREE MAIN CONSTRAINTS:

**1. MORNING** — Some people love the morning and can wake up early, while others are night owls. Some people have to be at work early or have kids to take to school and can't participate. You also have to be a certain type of person to set your alarm at 5:00 a.m. on a weekday morning, dress up in costume, and dance before going to work—we know it's not for everyone!

**2. SOBER** — Our events are sober, so a person who claims to not be able to dance or party without a drink in hand wouldn't like our events.

**3. DANCE + FITNESS** —Working out and dancing to electronic music with live instruments is an activity that requires a willingness to let go—you know if it's your thing, and if it's not.

# MAKE IT HAPPEN

Your turn! Define your Personal Core Values and the Core Values of your community. Then think about what you would like to see as the Constraints for your community or organization. Remember, it's not to keep people out, it's to help people know what they're in for!

**NOW, ON TO IDENTIFYING YOUR CORE COMMUNITY:** These are the special humans who give your community wings. When we launched Daybreaker, we invited a select group of FYFs to join our first few events and initially kept them private in order to establish a positive and energetic tone and vibe for our community from the start. We sat down over the course of several days, wrote out each friend's name, and thoughtfully debated who was an FYF and would be a good initial Core Community member. We curated and edited and thought hard about the mix of humans we were inviting and whether they would all get along and energize each other. It wasn't about packing the house with everyone and anyone. It wasn't about getting "hot models" to show up and objectifying them. It wasn't about inviting folks who had thousands of followers on social media. *It was all about energy.* We wanted to create a space that *felt* good. This is the definition of **Community Architecture**—*thoughtful energy curation.*

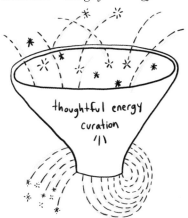

# THE BIG SECRET:

## When you get the right mix of

## ENERGY

## in a room, it's magic, and a flourishing community becomes inevitable.

Knowing how to curate a good energy mix is the key to launching a magnetic community. The thing is, you can't manufacture positive energy. You have to radiate it in order to attract it. This is why Going IN and understanding your Axis of Energy is so important as you begin to evaluate energy for your community.

## Good vibes want to be around good vibes.

Authentic and positive energy are what ultimately catapulted our Daybreaker community around the world.

# Things to consider about each potential Core Community member:

**ENERGY**—How's this person's energy? Positive? Vibrant? Inviting? Encouraging? Kind? Are they an FYF? What kind of energy do they bring to a room?

**PASSION**—Are they passionate about the community and the Core Values it embodies? Trust your gut. Someone may be passionate about your community but living on the left side of the Axis of Energy. If so, they're not the right energy for your Core Community.

**PERSONALITY MIX**—Consider a balance of personality types. For instance—joyful leaders, enthusiastic followers, maternal types (not always women!), funny people, some high energy, some calm energy, big-picture thinkers, make-it-happen types, etc. Think about whether the mix of people you're inviting will create the energy you envision for the community.

**PORTALS**—Portals share without any fear or insecurity and love to cheerlead new communities. Remember, Portals are not the same as social media influencers. On social media, anyone can follow you and it's mostly a one-way conversation. Portals are people who represent doorways to like-minded, authentic communities that you can actually belong to. Inviting Portals to join your initial Core Community will inspire more generous sharing.

Think about these four elements as you create your list of potential Core Community members!

## R—RITUAL

**DEFINING THE RITUALS AND TRADITIONS FOR YOUR COMMUNITY IS VITAL TO DEVELOPING LOYALTY AND A SENSE OF BELONGING.** You feel the most connected when you participate in something bigger than yourself. Rituals are how we connect to one another meaningfully. It's wearing the same sports jerseys as our parents and grandparents and knowing the same team cheers. It's singing "Happy Birthday" in unison. It's humming "ohmmmm" together in yoga class. It's all the rites from every religion, including prayer and chanting. It's even eating breakfast, lunch, and dinner together as a family—that's a ritual too.

When you participate in the traditions and rituals of a community, large or small, you inevitably feel a deeper connection to it.

Growing up, my parents created many rituals and traditions for our family. Tradition was steeped into the fabric of my parents' cultures and it was important to them that our family create our own. For example, rain or shine, on vacation or at home, social commitments or not—we ate as a family every Sunday. My parents were adamant about this ritual until we left for college. As much as we kicked and screamed at times, I now see the power of what they were modeling for us.

Choosing rituals requires thought and intention. Think about what traditions or rituals you want to adopt or create and why they are important to you, your friends, and your community. They also require **effort and participation** in seeing them through day to day, month to month, year to year.

RITUAL =

Intention
----- + -----
Participation

# MAKE IT HAPPEN

What rituals and traditions can you invite into your life, office, and community? Think about whether you want them to be meaningful, fun, inspiring, or productive. Try to make them simple and relatively easy to commit to doing every day or every week.

How will your members participate? How will their participation deepen their connection to this community?

# Rituals upon entry and exit of any gathering invite a deeper community experience.

**ENTRY AND EXIT RITUALS INSPIRE A SENSE OF COMMUNITY AND BELONGING.** Think of hellos and good-byes and how they make you feel. It's the handshake hello and the hugs good-bye that we remember, right? Yet we don't take the time to think about how we enter and exit a community or business experience. Instead we have receptionists, bouncers, and hostesses greeting us in similar ways, and rarely saying much more than a minimal farewell. What if the cashiers at the grocery store paid you a compliment as they bagged your groceries? Or what if the greeter at the movies told you jokes in line or gave you a secret handshake on your way in? What if, as you left, you were invited to put a wish in a mini-wishing well?

At all of Daybreaker's events, we've designed distinct Entry and Exit Rituals. Instead of mean bouncers looking you up and down, we have a "Hugging Committee." Every single person gets a hug and a "Good morning!" when they walk in. This creates instant camaraderie and releases oxytocin—the "O" in D.O.S.E., activated through human

touch. It's such a simple idea, but when it's early in the morning and everyone is still groggy, a warm and inviting hug is a wonderful way to wake up our community and get the cobwebs out. I've probably hugged over ten thousand community members at this point, and the number of people who have thanked me afterward and shared that they were nervous about going alone or were going through stuff and needed a hug continues to remind me why this ritual is so important. *It also reminded me that we don't hug each other enough!*

At the end of every Daybreaker, our exit ritual is reading intentions together. We hand out "Intention Cards" and read them together out loud as a community. Imagine six hundred community members reading a beautiful poem or quote out loud in unison to close a dance party where you just sweated for two hours and left it all on the dance floor. We stop the music fifteen minutes before the end of the party to do this ritual together—it's one of the most emotionally resonant moments at our events. It gives us something to hold on to as a group when we all part ways and head off to work.

It's also nice to give a token to your community members on their way out so they have something to hold on to, as so much of our life is digital, and a physical object can be more memorable and inspiring. Using all of our five senses inspires deeper connection.

# MAKE IT HAPPEN

Think of what rituals you could invite into the entrance and exit of your community gathering. And if you're open to sharing, I'd love to hear all about it at @love.radha and #belongbook!

## MORNING RITUAL IN JAPAN

Starting in 1928 and continuing in many parts of Japan today, Japan's national radio station (NHK) would broadcast *rajio taiso*, which means "Radio Exercise." When people tuned in at the appointed early morning hour, they'd hear a simple piano tune guided by a masculine voice directing them in ten minutes of calisthenics. Whether they were in school about to start class, at a car factory ready to assemble cars, or at the bank before the markets opened, they'd stop what they were doing and exercise together. I genuinely believe some of Japan's success as a country is attributable to this simple morning ritual that united the whole country. And it has certainly contributed to the long Japanese life span!

Growing up, my sisters and I went to Japanese school every Saturday. Before classes started, our whole school (several hundred Canadian–Japanese kids) did *rajio taiso* to wake up our bodies and get ready to learn. All these years later, while my Japanese has gotten rusty, I remember how connected I felt to my classmates each time we moved in unison before starting our day. So a few years ago, carrying forward the ritual, I introduced *rajio taiso* to our Daybreaker's HQ team. Now, just about every day at our office in Brooklyn, we do Japanese calisthenics together. At this point our whole team knows it by heart, and it's been an incredible way to create camaraderie in the office and get our blood pumping at 3 p.m.

## A—AESTHETICS

We often overlook the importance of aesthetics as it relates to attracting the right community members for you. Aesthetics *do* matter in community architecture. Colors, fonts, logo designs, materials, look, and feel all play an important role in creating community. Think about it: Why do doctors wear white coats? Or fans wear team jerseys? Or business folks wear fancy suits? We all wear costumes and assign meaning to what we wear and how we present ourselves. We believe in the aesthetics that have been assigned to our roles. It's no different if you're a community! Aesthetics give you a sense of familiarity that this is *your* community and that builds camaraderie. It also helps you to decide if the community is right for you. The name of your community also matters. It should be memorable, unique, and inviting. It can take some trial and error. Say it out loud again and again. Get other people

[LOGO]

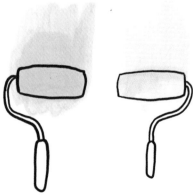

to say it. Make sure the words sound aesthetically pleasing to the ear. I've seen too many incredible leaders launch communities without a distinct aesthetic, and they often fail.

If you want to create a viable community, pay attention to design. At Daybreaker, we spent weeks defining our color palettes, fonts, logos, and design aesthetic. Aesthetics take design into account in both two and three dimensions and include the spaces in which we gather. The question to ask when thinking about aesthetics is **"How will this make someone *feel*?"** It all goes back to energy. What kind of energy will the aesthetics of your community inspire?

# MAKE IT HAPPEN

Define the aesthetics of your community. Think about what you're designing—from the sound of the name of your community to your logo and where that logo will appear (website, business cards, T-shirts, etc.). Do you want to communicate excitement, empathy, trust? After you've determined the feeling, think about the look of it—colors, fonts, applications, and space. If you'd like help with the name, talk to someone who tends to be articulate and creative with words. For help with the look of your community, find someone whose clothing style or home decor you admire. A sense of style tends to run through all the visuals in a person's life, so it should be easy to spot.

## W—WHY + WHAT?

When I'm advising on building a community, I always start the conversation with these five questions:

**1.** Why do _you_ care?

**2.** Why are you the right person to lead this community?

**3.** Why should this community exist?

**4.** What other communities or affinity groups can you align with?

**5.** Why will this community be sustainable over time?

### 1. Why do _you_ care?

Why is this community important to _you_? Can you stay excited about this community for a long time? Every successful Community Architect I meet has a story about why their community matters to them. For example, my friend Jesse became deeply passionate about meditation after seeing the healing powers of the practice in his own life (overcoming anxiety), so he took it upon himself to organize group meet-ups for his friends to meditate together every month. His passion and dedication were contagious, and friends shared his meet-ups with other friends. Within months, he had built a community of several thousand meditators in New York City and launched a meditation community called Medi Club, which continues to thrive today. When your passion is authentic and clear, your community feels it and wants to be a part of it.

## 2. Why are you the right person to lead this community? Are you the trusted messenger?

You probably know the answer to this in your gut, but ask yourself the questions anyway.

Are you willing to do the work it takes? Do you have the stamina and the passion? Gently acknowledge if you're operating from a place of insecurity or fear (Red Ego) or if you're ready to listen to your Green Ego, which is focused on generosity and abundance.

Write down three to five good reasons why you would crush it as a comunity leader. Prop yourself up! Brag about yourself!

Gently recognize if your reasons for starting a community are truly authentic. What are your motives? If it's only to make money, it will never work. If it's because you're hanging out with the Mean Girls and are comparing yourself to others and want to create a community because your arch nemesis is, it will never work either. It has to be pure and authentic for it to really work.

# FOOD FOR THOUGHT:

Our biggest limitation is fear, and it's not real. Fear is made up in our heads. Fear and empathy in many ways are BFFs. Sometimes, the more we care about others and the bigger our hearts, the more fear holds us back because we don't want to disappoint. How can we lead a life that is both empathetic and fearless?

Chew on that for a second.

### 3. Why should this community exist?
### (What is the purpose of this community?)

There's an important distinction between why a community is important *to you* and why it should exist *in the world*. Ask yourself, "What purpose does this community fulfill for my neighborhood, or for the world?" What is the ultimate goal of this community?

There is a wonderful community called the NEXUS Global Youth Summit. The purpose of this community has been crystal clear from the start: The children of the wealthiest humans on the planet will inherit trillions of dollars from their parents over the next twenty years. Many of them have expressed interest in funding projects that will benefit the planet and *all* the humans on it—not just the top 1 percent. NEXUS helps pair young, wealthy inheritors with social entrepreneurs who are building these world-changing businesses and organizations. The NEXUS community now has thousands of members globally and hosts an annual summit at the United Nations in New York City. When a community has a specific goal with a clear mission in mind led by passionate Community Architects, it catches fire.

## 4. What other communities or affinity groups can you align with?

As everything takes inspiration from other things, there are hundreds of communities and affinity groups that could be complementary to your community. If you want to start a "Tea drinking community that reads Shakespeare," the obvious communities to connect with are tea drinking groups and Shakespeare groups. There are 442 tea groups happening right now around the world on meetup.com alone! Start exploring and participating. Refresh your Four Stages of Community.

## 5. Why will this community be sustainable over time?

Do you have a long-term plan in place for your community? How are you evolving? The best communities think about the present and the future. In order to keep going, we built a robust organization for Daybreaker with a comprehensive training manual and a well-organized team in Brooklyn. While community can feel like a squishy concept, it requires systemization to grow and sustain. Every community is uniquely different, and as such, all systems require thoughtful execution.

## L—LANGUAGE

Language is our most powerful form of communication, yet we don't always have the necessary vocabulary.

**I USED TO THINK "WORDS" AND "LANGUAGE" MEANT ESSENTIALLY THE SAME THING, UNTIL IT HIT ME:**

**Words** are a collection of letters that convey *meaning* so we *understand* each other, while **language** conveys *energy* so we *feel* each other. Energy—which in the case of spoken language includes tone—often gets lost on email. We hastily and thoughtlessly text one another, using emojis to replace language. We easily get hurt and inflamed because we have lost our language sophistication in our quest to simplify, emojify, and swipe. I've had my feelings hurt and have unintentionally hurt feelings too, in my hasty "doing seventeen things at once" text messages to friends and colleagues. I'll reread texts that I sent to frustrated or upset friends and not recognize myself in the exchange. As a student of efficiency who gets excited when I'm showering and brushing my teeth at the same time, I started thinking about taking a breath before sending a message to check in on my energy and language.

We are complex creatures and when we oversimplify and minimize language, we hobble communication. Recently I reread letters I wrote to friends and lovers when I was twenty years old—before smartphones, Facebook, or any social media came into the world—and I was astonished at the difference of depth of feeling in my writing compared to my one emoji thumbs-up responses today. Since there's no denying the benefits and the convenience of our smartphones, my question becomes:

# "How can we honor technology and the incredible opportunities it offers us while continuing to develop the potential of human language?"

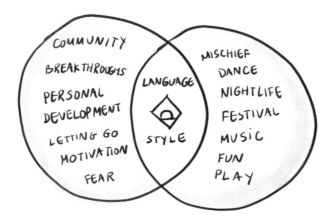

Our MC, Elliot, is the Voice of Daybreaker. We have long discussions about language style. Before events, we think through how to share our collective message on the dance floor in a way that feels thoughtful, fun, and authentic, and will inspire our community to *let go*. We can't be too preachy. We can't expect everyone to come to the dance floor with the same energy, so we have to be inviting and encouraging to those who are more tentative and also honor those who are ready to *daaance*. To figure this out, we looked at our Core Community, did a deep dive into our Core Values, and created a language style that married the worlds of nightlife and personal development. As such we include language that's inspiring, fun, and encouraging as well as language that's underground, mysterious, mischievous, self-expressive, and thematic.

It's not always about being succinct and efficient. It's about how the words flow together to create a language style that makes someone *feel* the intended feeling. It all starts with intention.

My simple rule of thumb in developing a language style: Split the difference between what you want to say as a human, artist, or community and what your community longs for in their lives. When you define your Core Community and Constraints, you will know whom you're talking to. If you're only ever catering to yourself and don't care about your community or audience, it will be tough to grow your community. And if you only cater to what others want to hear, you won't convey your personal passion and vision. Your messaging will be vanilla and "safe."

HERE'S MY CHALLENGE TO YOU: Define your language style for your community today, including *why* that style is right for your community. Think about how words matter but also how language is even more influential.

# CRAWL
# in a nutshell:

**C**

### DEFINE YOUR CORE VALUES + CONSTRAINTS + CORE COMMUNITY

Create the philosophical foundation for your community.

**R**

### CREATE RITUALS!

What are the rituals for your community?

How will your community participate?

**A**

### DEFINE YOUR AESTHETIC

What does your logo look like? Fonts? Color palette?

Do you have a memorable and inviting name?

**W**

### WHY + WHAT

Answer the five questions honestly. It will determine the potential for strength and endurance for the community and for you as a leader.

**L**

### WHAT'S YOUR LANGUAGE STYLE?

How are you speaking to your community? Remember to combine what you want to say with what your community wants for their lives.

A community, like a garden, needs consistent nurturing and loving attention.

# CHAPTER 7

# ℕurture Your Community

## Ten Foolproof Ways to Keep Them Coming Back for More

think of creating new friendships and communities in similar ways to planting a garden. The first several months require the most dedication, care, nurture, and support before the plants are strong enough to survive and multiply on their own. Then, as the garden grows, new variables are introduced and we adapt. As long as the garden exists and continues to grow and evolve, it requires thoughtful tending, with weekly waterings and monthly prunings. It's a great metaphor for community building. There's no time for playing hard-to-get and being "too cool for school" here. Your plants won't survive! Following are ten foolproof ways to nurture your community that have served me.

# 1. Be Present and Listen

**WITH ALL THE DIGITAL DISTRACTIONS IN THE WORLD TODAY, HUMANS CRAVE CONNECTION.** If you show interest in other humans and get excited about *their* lives, they will want to keep hanging out with you. You can feel when someone is paying attention to you, and it feels good! Also, share praise and pay compliments where it feels authentic. Don't hold back compliments out of shyness or potential awkwardness. To hear a genuine compliment just feels good—for both the giver and the receiver. But even more than that, focus on the beauty of simply being present for the other person. Dropping in, sharing praise, and *truly* listening. *If you can do this, you'll have friends for life.*

## 2. TAKE INITIATIVE AND BE ACCOUNTABLE

**COMMUNITY IS BUILT ON INTENTION, ENERGY, AND
ACTION.** Have the courage to reach out! Be proactive and true
to your word. Don't be flaky. Accountability is key to building
community. We live in a time where we cancel on each other, have
a hard time "committing," and wait for others to "do it first." Have
the courage and keep taking initiative! When you are dedicated to
showing up daily, weekly, or monthly, your friends and community
can count on that and, in turn, will start showing up for you too. At
Daybreaker, we have dedicated ourselves to showing up monthly
for our community to dance, connect, and self-express before going
to work. We take our community presence very seriously, and this
accountability has helped us grow to twenty-five cities across the
world in less than four years. People want to be a part of something
they can count on. And then that community reenergizes *us* when we
are tired or down. It's a beautiful cycle. So show up and be present
when you do. Your community will recognize that and
will be loyal to you too.

## 3. EAT TOGETHER

**FOOD IS AN ESSENTIAL PART OF LIFE AND VITAL TO COMMUNITY BUILDING.** We gather around food for every aspect of life, from family meals to sports, weddings, camping trips, birthday parties, festivals, and everything in between. Taking hospitality and food seriously are surefire ways to nurture and sustain your community. And it's one of the ways to be a Five Sense Friend! Getting creative with food can include a beautiful dinner party, but it can also be as simple as snacks for a meeting. Even if cooking isn't your thing, find a way to convey love, respect, and commitment by having a little something to eat together.

**Some ideas:**

- **A COMMUNAL QUESTION.** My best friend Max hosts dinner parties where he has prepared questions ahead of time. He lets everyone know that part of the dinner conversation will be dedicated to the question, allowing each person to share with the whole table, rather than with just the person next to them. In every case, it has led to a more connected experience. Having a few questions to choose from and deciding which ones to use based on the energy of the group will make for a more connected conversation. There's a wonderful community-building card game called "Vulnerability Is Sexy," which tees up interesting questions to break the ice and go deeper with one another.

● **DO IT TOGETHER.** Another idea is preparing a meal together—setting the table, chopping veggies, and cleaning up inspire teamwork and belonging through participation, and I've seen many strangers become friends through this. Often, Eli and I will only buy ingredients from the grocery store for our dinner parties so everyone can participate in creating the meal together.

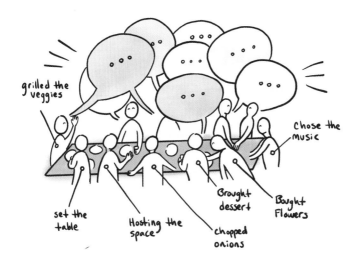

● **BLACK TIE TUESDAY.** Two of my dear friends and I organize a "Black Tie Tuesday" dinner every few months. Life is far more fun when you change it up! Alfredo, Philip, Eli, and I invite friends to dress up in fancy attire to eat at a casual restaurant. It's hilarious for everyone involved—including the waiters and bartenders! Try it!

## 4. GIVE GIFTS

**GIVING GIFTS SHOWS THOUGHTFULNESS AND INTENTION, AND THAT GOES A *LOOOONG* WAY.**
Imagine walking into a conference room and instead of just boring white tables and a PowerPoint presentation, there was a scroll wrapped with a ribbon at every seat, containing a playful poem reflecting the values of the company. Or what if you started working at a new company and before your first day of work, three team members sent you a playlist to listen to on your way to work, a book to read, or breakfast treats to fuel you for your first few days! Our friend Jesse recently sent Eli and me hot sauce in the mail. He knew that Eli loves to cook (and I love to eat!) and out of the blue he sent us the most amazing hot sauce from the city he was traveling to for work. We were so touched by this that we must have told twenty different people, and now they think of Jesse as a great guy. Another friend, Molly, recently sent me a beautiful handwritten card in the mail just to share encouragement to get through this very book! I welled up receiving it. While I'm also grateful to friends who have sent emails and text messages showing support, the gift of Molly's time and intention was especially moving. These things cost next to nothing and foster a sense of belonging that reverberates through the whole group.

# 5. Inspire Fun, Play, and Adventure

**WHEN YOU INSPIRE YOUR FRIENDS AND COMMUNITY TO BE MORE PLAYFUL AND GO ON ADVENTURES, PEOPLE WANT YOU AROUND.** Being "serious" and "grown up" are overrated. When we were younger, most of us were happy and carefree and laughed more easily! Work on bringing that to your community.

**Some ideas:**

- **PUMPKINS.** My friend David invited me to brunch one day around Halloween. Before we ordered our meal at the restaurant, he dug into his jacket pocket, pulled out a miniature pumpkin, and set it on the table. I looked at him quizzically and asked what it was for. He looked back at me with a twinkle in his eye and said, "What do you mean? It's table garnish!" I almost fell off my chair. It was so ridiculous, random, and fun! The next time I saw him, he brought pinecones to my office and lovingly placed them around my desk. Now, every time I see him, my tail wags.

- **CROWNS.** Another story that goes down as a textbook example of a playful couple is one about Sofija and Ben. The first time we met, they came to dinner as guests of two dear friends. Instead of being shy and demure, they brought kits to make paper crowns. Ben and Sofija run a successful business, but instead of talking about the stock market and their 401(k) plans, we spent an hour making paper crowns and trying them on and laughing hysterically. These are friends you want around!

- **GOLD STARS.** The last and simplest idea is . . . gold stars. They never get old. When Eli and I visited his dad at the hospital during a procedure, we gave gold stars to all the nurses and doctors who took care of him, saying, "Thank you for being so awesome. You just earned a gold star!" They were genuinely excited to receive their stars and even put them on their hospital badges. The atmosphere at the hospital instantly became lighter and less stressful. It's the little things that matter. Take initiative and be courageously silly!

## 6. DESIGN SPACES FOR BELONGING

**HOME FEELS LIKE HOME BECAUSE OF THE INTENTION, LOVE, AND CARE THAT YOU PUT INTO IT.** When you create thoughtful and intentional spaces that people want to gather in, they'll keep coming back. My parents' house is simple yet beautiful, especially at Christmas, when my mom and dad hang twinkly lights, place garlands on each banister, and decorate the tree with every (and I mean every) ornament we've made since we were kids. To this day, my mother has created a space that *feels* good, and I look forward to coming home every chance I get.

*Designing intentional spaces is at the root of belonging.* It's the physical container for relationships to form and deepen. My friend Tony Hsieh is the CEO of Zappos. He designed his office to inspire more "collisions" in the hallways; Google built a cafeteria for the employees to connect over meals; and SoulCycle designed their locker rooms so that those coming into the spin studio have to walk past those who have just finished a class. Thoughtful spaces will inspire deeper, more meaningful connections on all sides.

**What's up with couches?** When my twin sister, Miki, and I were living together as roommates, we discovered that couches were awkward for eye-contact conversations. You have to crane your neck uncomfortably to talk to each other! So we got rid of ours and built a cuddle-puddle in our living room instead. We had two queen-size mattresses that we pushed together with pillows and throws adorning them, and when friends came over, we cuddle-puddled together, talking, laughing, and watching movies. We've had friends in their sixties down to our three-year-old niece cuddle-puddling in our living room, and it's been the best way to connect as FSFs!

When you live in an apartment, typically a couch sits on one wall and a TV sits across on the other wall. This is the inherent problem with city apartments. Think about it: Couches are angular and linear and are not conducive to a community experience. They're made to watch TV or read a book. It's difficult to have a conversation with eye contact on a couch. L-shaped or facing couches are better, and circular couches or cuddle-puddles (or boudoirs) like the one Miki and I had are the best for connecting!

**Tips on designing spaces:**

● **THE BOWL EFFECT**—At Daybreaker, we look for spaces that are bowl-shaped and have multilevels so our community can dance together and make eye contact with one another. We call it the Bowl Effect—circular seating (and dancing!) areas inspire a deeper sense of intimacy and belonging. Try it! Flat, rectangular surfaces are more . . . flat.

- **LIGHTING IS KEY**—Don't underestimate the importance of "vibe." Think about what mood you want to set for your gathering. Lighting can define the experience. Candles, dimmers, natural light, and special light bulbs (try a few) are great. Plants, greenery, flowers, pillows, throws, incense, and candles are also your friends. If you activate all five senses (Five Sense Friends!), you'll inspire a deeper sense of belonging.

## 7. ADVANCED COMMUNICATION

**MY BROTHER-IN-LAW ANDREW IS AN EXPERT ON THE ART OF MEANINGFUL CONVERSATION.** I've watched him get engrossed in conversation with a stranger in the middle of a thousand-person dance party with thumping electronic music (not kidding). He has an uncanny ability to assess an environment and ask the right question at the right moment. He says, "A reality that we should all embrace is that our professional success, career trajectory, friendships, and romantic relationships can change dramatically because of a single conversation." Here are some tips he shares:

**Find your Authentic Voice.** The Authentic Voice can be defined as a deep-down understanding of who we are, what we want, and what we believe in. If we don't know what our voice is, we'll constantly seek validation from others to tell us what is "acceptable" or "cool." Think about the things that truly matter to you. This is what makes up your voice.

Your Authentic Voice

Personal History

Purpose Values Interests Abilities V.I.A.

**Ask better questions!** No more "What do you do?" Asking thoughtful questions and listening to the responses will make anyone you're talking to feel valued. Try having a full conversation without bringing up work.

**Five questions that beat "What do you do?"**

What are you most excited about?

What are you finding challenging right now?

What's the first birthday memory you have?

What do you spend most of your time thinking about these days?

If you could do anything, what would you be doing?

# MAKE IT HAPPEN

Go DEEP with a friend, family member, or coworker you've been wanting to get to know better— or get reacquainted with. Set aside time for a meal, hangout, or train ride, and practice these methods. The more we get into each other's backpacks, the more belonging, empathy, and connection we will feel to one another.

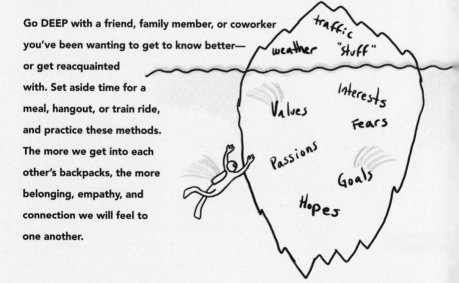

# MAKE IT HAPPEN

Next time you're talking to a friend you know well, make a conscious effort to touch their arm, hand, or leg when you talk to them. Try hugging rather than handshaking (although handshaking is better than nothing!). Really focus on being an FSF (Five Sense Friend). Even if it's awkward at first, give it a shot. If you invite more affection into your relationship, your friend will more than likely respond positively! It's clinically proven that touching one another soothes our nervous systems, supports our immune systems, and makes us healthier and happier. The more you practice being affectionate, the easier and more fluid it will become. And the better it will feel! Just don't make it creepy!

## 8. Touch Your Friends More

**TOUCH AND AFFECTION RELEASE OXYTOCIN (THE "O" IN D.O.S.E.!)** and inspire a sense of belonging, yet we rarely touch each other in a friendly, casual way. Most of us focus all of our affection and intimacy toward our romantic partners. It's wild that Americans watch the most porn of any country in the world (40 percent of the most-watched porn sites around the world are from Americans!),* yet we are physically starved for affection. I said it earlier, but it bears repeating that a study showed that, in conversation, Mexicans touched each other an average of 185 times in one sitting, while in Florida, they touched each other only twice. That's part of why I love dancing, because you're naturally holding on to your friend while you dance or bumping into each other as you jump around.

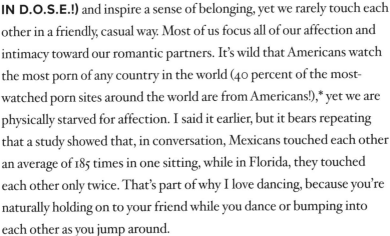

*Pornhub, "2017 Year in Review," pornhub.com/insights/2017-year-review.

## 9. Dress Up in Costumes

**LIFE IS WAY MORE FUN WHEN WE MAKE EXCUSES TO DRESS UP.** At Daybreaker, we have a theme at every event to inspire more play and connection. When you dress up together, there's a camaraderie that's created and you feel a deeper sense of belonging. It's also creative in a way that's outside of most people's comfort zone, which is good! It gives you a chance to laugh at yourself, admire others' creativity, and start conversations. It's a kind of fun that brings out the child in everyone, and I love seeing people be vulnerable, silly, and then more confident when they dress up.

## 10. Get Active Together

**THIS ONE IS OBVIOUS BUT STILL NEEDS TO BE CALLED OUT.** Work out, play sports, go for hikes, and dance! Participating in activities and taking initiative to plan activities with your friends are surefire ways to keep your community coming back for more. If you like hiking, plan hikes for your community— and bring gold stars and paper crowns!

The big secret to keeping community alive is to give, give, give. Have the courage to create and invite others to participate. When you do, the world will open up to you.

My ultimate motto for nurturing and sustaining communities is, "What you put in is what you get out." It's that simple.

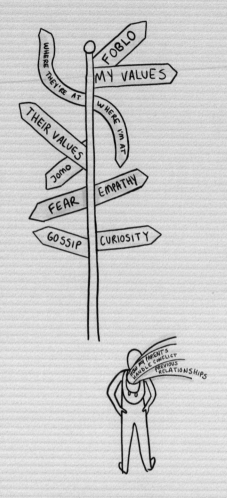

How we choose to embrace inevitable conflict will shape all our relationships.

# CHAPTER 8

# Reframe and Embrace Conflict

## Life Languages, the Friendship Cycle, Avoiding FOBLO, and Eradicating Gossip

This is where the rubber meets the road. Conflict, and dealing with it gracefully, is Community Architecture 2.0. As a sensitive and passionate half-Indian, half-Japanese, French Canadian woman, this is where I've struggled the most. Fire courses through my veins, and there's no question that my parents (specifically my dad—hi, Dad!) set the tone for how I deal with conflict. It's been my biggest challenge and I've synthesized the lessons I've learned over the years into the big ideas that follow. They've helped me *tremendously*, and I hope they will lessen the struggle of inevitable conflict for you.

## EMPATHY FIRST

I often feel misunderstood. As an employer and a CEO, everything
I say is recorded and taken seriously. I'm certainly not always right,
and I often say the wrong thing. If I'm trying to give constructive
feedback to a team member when I haven't eaten lunch, have a
meeting with my accountant in an hour, and have three people texting
and calling me at the same time, it's hard for the words to come out
in the way I want them to. Also, my team member may be going
through stuff too and will be receiving my feedback differently than I
intended based on a host of reasons.

We forget that there's more to every
conversation than the one we're actually
having.

## LIFE LANGUAGE

My friend and fellow Community Architect David (the one who
brought the pumpkin to lunch!) and I spent an afternoon at my office
workshopping all the ways we could deal with conflict personally and
professionally. We both run companies and deal with personalities
every day, so it was an especially productive and interesting
conversation. What we realized is that it's not about conflict
resolution itself—*it's about considering where each person is when
they're coming into a conversation in the first place.*

Since then, I've spent months refining our brainstorm into three questions that I call our *Life Language*—it's a simple language for how to approach any life conversation and have more empathy and understanding for where the person is before you meet them. Consider the following three questions *before* you enter any conversation with your friend, employee, colleague, or community member, and remember that these three questions are applicable to both of you, so you have six variables to consider:

**1. WHERE AM I *IN LIFE*?**—What does your overall life picture look like right now? Health? Finances? Family? Community? Job? Did you just relocate? Break up with a boyfriend? Lose your job? Get a new job? What's in your backpack?

**2. WHERE AM I *RIGHT NOW*?**—How's your state of mind in the present moment? How's your human meat suit doing? Are you hungry? Are you stressed? Did you just have a fight with a loved one this morning? Are you late for your meeting?

**3. WHERE AM I *WITH YOU*?**—How's our relationship? Are we getting along right now? Are we tense? Do I feel betrayed or hurt? How well do we know each other? Am I at ease? Nervous? Are you someone I admire?

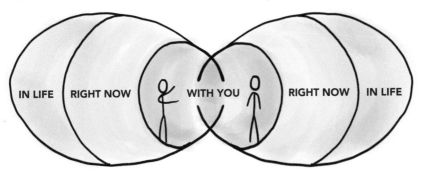

IN LIFE | RIGHT NOW | WITH YOU | RIGHT NOW | IN LIFE

I've certainly been in many conversations in which each of these Life Language questions was impacting the conversation on both sides but neither of us addressed it. When we're not seeing, sharing, or even considering the full picture, misunderstanding happens. Society has placed so many rules on what should be shared and what is oversharing, what is appropriate and inappropriate, and we all have different interpretations based on our upbringing and past experiences. The more open and vulnerable we are with one another, the more we will understand each other and the more connected we will feel. As soon as I realized this, I started giving myself and anyone I was interacting with permission to be open with these questions. We would share where we were in life, in the moment and with each other. It allowed any tension or discomfort to just lift. Now, when a team member (or any friend) shares that they're PMS-ing or didn't get enough sleep the night before and are feeling tired, or they got into an argument with their mom, I know how best to communicate with them. We have built an office culture where we don't abuse this freedom or use it as an excuse to stay at home or do a poor job, but we can cry in front of each other (as CEO—Chief Emotional Officer, I cry all the time) and can share our feelings passionately without holding things against one another. Communication can be messy, and the more we understand each other's Life Language, the more empathy, belonging, and connection we will feel.

# MAKE IT HAPPEN

This week, go into all conversations thinking about these three questions on both sides, and have the courage and vulnerability to share your Life Language with that person and see what happens!

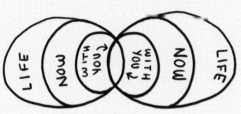

## FOMO, FOBLO, AND JOMO

We all know and have felt *FOMO—Fear of Missing Out*. When friends post on social media that they went somewhere and you had the opportunity to go but didn't, you think, "Ahhhh, I wish I could have been there!" That's the *fun* kind of FOMO—the one you could have gone to but *chose* not to go. Of course, there's the FOMO in which you feel it's probably not a good idea to go, but you go because you just don't want to miss out. That can be great, or it can rule your life. FOMO gets managed the more you know your own colorful rainbow and get comfortable with yourself.

The FOMO we're all ashamed of talking about is *FOBLO— Fear of Being Left Out*. Being left out at any age is painful and makes us want to crawl into our beds and ask ourselves if all our friends hate us. *Why weren't we invited?* As pack animals, we like to be included. Yet we never talk about it when we're left out. Pride gets in the way. We resent or talk negatively about the person who didn't invite us. We make up stories in our own heads. Social media has also made

# FOMO, FOBLO, and JOMO

**JOMO**

**JOY OF MISSING OUT**
High sense of belonging
High self-esteem.
You're genuinely happy
to do your own thing.

**FOMO**

**FEAR OF MISSING OUT**
Mid-level sense of belonging
Confidence in your friendships, but
pangs of envy from not being there.

**FOBLO**

**FEAR OF BEING LEFT OUT**
Low sense of belonging
Low self-esteem. Painful, unhealthy, and reversible!

FOBLO very real. We can see everything that we weren't invited to, and it can hurt when friends we care about are involved. It's why studies have shown that scrolling through social media makes us less happy. Studies have also shown that our brain processes pain from rejection in the same way it processes physical pain, like having a broken bone. Social rejection can also bring on feelings of depression, anger, sadness, anxiety, and jealousy.

If it's so common, why is being left out so shameful and, as my British friend Philip says, "not to be talked about"? What if we made #FOBLO a thing we acknowledged? Let's take out the shame and talk about it. ***But also, FOBLO can be reversed!***

## HERE ARE NINE WAYS TO OVERCOME FOBLO:

**ASK YOURSELF WHY YOU'RE FEELING FOBLO IN THE FIRST PLACE.** We typically ignore painful feelings, busy ourselves, and pretend they're not there instead of acknowledging them. But when you don't acknowledge your feelings, they become amplified and you end up getting more upset. Once you actually face your feelings, you may realize, "Wait a minute, I rarely hang out with or call this person, why would they invite me?" or "What am I getting so upset about? It's *one* event. I'm exactly where I'm supposed to be." It may be human nature to imagine the worst—"They don't care about me!"—but being objective about reality is often much simpler and more empowering. If it's still bothering you, get Gently Self-Aware about how you've been showing up for this friend. Are you often negative?

A shit-talker? Or positive and participatory? When you're together, are you making an effort to connect? If you're not part of their day-to-day life and aren't checking in regularly, chances are it's not about you! And if they're maliciously excluding you to make you feel bad, *they* are the ones who will feel bad in the end, because that behavior always catches up with the perpetrator.

**TALK ABOUT IT! BE VULNERABLE.** Send your friend a note that says "#FOBLO—did you forget about me?" Bring it up courageously and share your feelings without accusing them.

**REMEMBER: IT'S NOT ALWAYS ABOUT YOU!** Sometimes, humans just want to hang out with other humans, and that's totally cool. It can be freeing to realize that you're not the center of the universe. Do your own thing! The world is exciting—new adventures await.

**YOU'RE EXACTLY WHERE YOU'RE SUPPOSED TO BE.** Yes, it's a bit philosophical, but when you recognize your awesomeness, hang out with your cheerleading Green Ego, and know that the energy was meant to flow this way, you'll find that it's incredibly liberating to *know that you're exactly where you're supposed to be.*

**CHECK IN WITH YOUR SELF-ESTEEM.** When we don't know our own self-worth and we depend on others to feel good about ourselves, this is when we experience FOBLO the most. Recognize your unique gifts and go find something else to do! Go back to the gratitude exercise in Chapter 3 and think of three things you're grateful for in this moment.

**FOCUS ON SELF-CARE.** Release your D.O.S.E.! Exercise, dance in front of the mirror, take a hot bath, call someone, go get a juice, meditate, meet up with other friends. This is YOUR time now— create your own beautiful moment.

**RELEASE ALL EXPECTATIONS.** When you have expectations, you're going to feel resentful and will experience FOBLO. *Expectations are resentments waiting to happen.* Also, think about what level in the Four Stages of Community you're in with this friend. If someone in your Inner Core Community makes you feel FOBLO regularly, it's time to think about whether this person should be in your Inner Core. You should feel comfortable enough to call them and honestly ask, "Hey,  was there a reason I wasn't invited?" If it's anyone from your Exploratory, Participatory, or Outer Core Community who hasn't invited you, you shouldn't have any expectations to be invited.

**THROW YOUR OWN DINNER PARTY OR EVENT!** A fellow Community Architect, Alison, and I always joke around about this: We create community for two reasons—to connect the world and so we're not left out! Hosts don't feel FOBLO by definition. So create your own experience and be courageously inclusive of even those who didn't include you. Your world will open up.

**USE FOBLO AS A LESSON.** Maybe you didn't realize how much this friend meant to you, and this feeling is a clue that you want to get closer. If you didn't care, you wouldn't feel FOBLO in the first place! Use this experience to inspire you to reach out in the future and connect more meaningfully.

When you overcome FOBLO, you will experience *JOMO—Joy of Missing Out*. You're happy and content to be exactly where you are.

Also, sometimes the best way to get over feeling FOBLO is to make others feel welcomed and included. Go out of your way to make an experience better. Don't just show up, show up with an FYF attitude. Go back to Chapter 7 and refresh yourself on the things you can do to enhance any experience! Bring food and playful gifts!

## THE FRIENDSHIP CYCLE

As someone who is naturally nostalgic, I've had to learn the beauty of the fact that all friendships evolve. My nostalgia has led me to some heartache about the way friendships have changed, but as I studied it in society and in my life and my friends' lives, I observed five phases that most friendships cycle through—what I call the *Friendship Cycle*. The goal is for you to know that you're not alone in feeling all these things and that friendships naturally go through life cycles. Not every friendship goes through every stage, and that's fine too.

### Gestation

To even get to the Gestation phase, you want to feel an Equal Energy Exchange. It exists in a brand-new relationship that you're excited about and actively want to invest in. These friendships are rare, so gut-check here. Don't go through this Friendship Cycle with just anyone. It takes a lot of emotional energy (and life is

# The Friendship Cycle

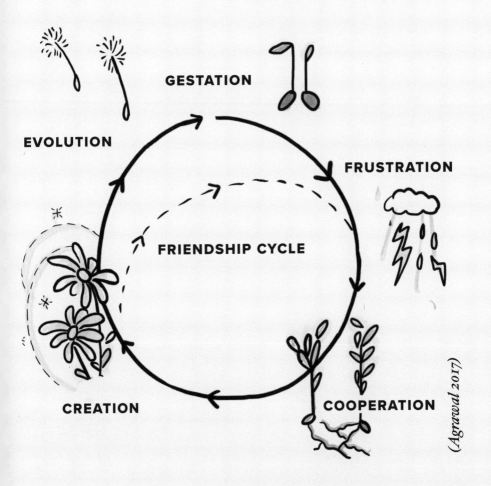

GESTATION

EVOLUTION

FRUSTRATION

FRIENDSHIP CYCLE

CREATION

COOPERATION

(Agrawal 2017)

busy with family, school, work, kids, etc.), so choose wisely! This stage is when you've met a new friend who aligns with your values and interests, really sees you for who you are, and fills up your tank. You're shiny-eyed and everything is rosy and fun and exciting and new! You have a new friend!

## Frustration

This is the phase where we get past our "best behavior" and begin forming real opinions about our new friend and start establishing our authentic voice in the relationship. Maybe you get into an argument about political beliefs. You see something about your new friend that rubs you the wrong way. Know that this is natural!! We lose a little excitement at this phase and are ready to challenge each other to establish the boundaries of our relationship. Unless we take the time and explore each other's Life Languages, it can sometimes end the friendship. Our Red Egos, which are fearful and competitive, can take over and we start hanging out with the Mean Girls, judging and comparing ourselves to our new friend. It takes patience, curiosity, communication, vulnerability, courage, and intention to get through this phase and recognize the beauty and rarity of this magical friendship.

**Don't run away.** Get curious, Go IN,

and do the work to gently go through your own stuff. If this person filled up your Energy Tank and you felt an authentic connection, trust your animal instinct and don't throw in the towel too easily.

The best antidote for frustration and conflict is *acknowledgment*. Let your Red Ego go and acknowledge your friend's feelings by first empathizing with what they're experiencing and then share your feelings vulnerably. We're all learning and growing! Challenge each other to look at the present and the future. Don't reread text messages from the past—in fact, don't use texting for a sensitive subject. Not only is tone lost in texting, but then you have a written record of how you are feeling *just* in that moment, which may change right after you hit send. Talk to your friend human to human!

*Note:* In rare cases, we can skip the Frustration phase and go straight to Cooperation!

## Cooperation

This sounds good, right? It is! It's when we take real time to get to know each other and understand, respect, and embrace our differences. We've successfully moved through the Frustration phase and can start trusting each other. We are energized by the friendship and our joy is greater than in the Gestation period because we've been through conflict and come out on the other side. We start spending more time together and feel an Equal Energy Exchange again. This is the stage of bonding, adventures, and deeper satisfaction.

### Creation

# This phase is magic!

It's our highest-energy phase. We feel creative energy in our trust and respect for one another. We're hanging out with our Green Egos and Soul Sisters and are ready to take on the world. This phase moves beyond the fun of hanging out. When you create something with a deep, true friend with whom you've overcome conflict successfully, the rewards fill your life. Whatever you've heard about not creating or being in business with friends is silly and a thing of the past. No matter what, we're going to evolve anyway, so why not create stuff together? Life is far more interesting and exciting when you do! That said, the Creation phase is always trial and error. Sometimes you will work seamlessly together, and other times the Frustration phase recurs more often than what you're comfortable with. Communication and acknowledgment will always help you through this.

### Evolution

As with everything in life, nothing stays the same. All communities and relationships evolve and change. When you sense it happening, rather than thinking, "This isn't what it used to be," consider this: It's never supposed to be what "it used to be"! Everything evolves, including communities and relationships, and it's a beautiful thing! Let's learn to embrace that!

Our summer intern, Jenny, asked me, "How do I know when it's time to move on from a friendship?" We talked for a while, and I told her what has worked for me. I check in with my Personal Core Values and ask if the friendship is continuing to align with them, and I apply the 80/20 rule. If 80 percent of the time you spend together feels like an Equal Energy Exchange and your tank is filled up, then keep investing in this relationship.

When I went deeper with Jenny, I learned that she also compared herself to her friend and felt neglected and not prioritized by her. She was still in the Frustration phase of her Friendship Cycle. Recognize what phase of your relationship you're in! It's on you to get curious as to why you're feeling negatively in the first place and have the courage to talk about it with your friend in person.

Some friendships will evolve together beautifully and bring you closer together and some will naturally drift apart. I used to get really sad when friends evolved in different directions, and mourning is a natural thing for us sensitive humans. But now I focus on gratitude for the time we had together and am excited for our respective journeys, whatever direction they take! They may even take you back to the Gestation phase with the same friend, later on. But there will also be someone new you can do this with. Ideally, we go around and around the Friendship Cycle all our lives.

Ultimately, when you go through the Friendship Cycle, you will feel a deeper sense of belonging with your friend and community.

## POOR SOIL FOR GROWTH: COMMUNICATING THROUGH SCREENS

If you've noticed a theme I return to, it's that screens are not always the best communication tool. When we communicate this way, we don't have the full picture. We don't know the person's emotional state, where they are, and how they're receiving our texts. What if someone you're texting from a taxi is caught in a hurricane in Florida? When we communicate in person, or at least by voice, we can feel immediate energetic reactions. Communicating through screens where we can't see each other limits understanding and empathy. If you are dealing with a conflict by text and email, acknowledge that you're bringing a whole new set of challenges to the issue.

**If you must proceed through texting, take these things into account:**

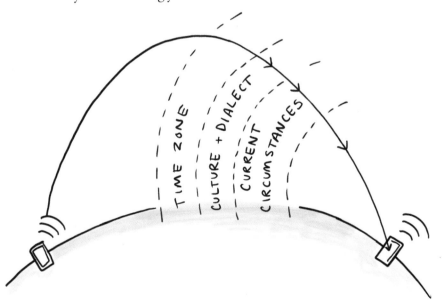

- When and where your friend is when sending you a message.

- Whether your words are properly translating your authentic energy and how you *actually* feel. Take your time, reread, and breathe before you press send on a text message!

- Whether your energy is organized or disorganized based on your physical state. (Are you hungry? Tired? Stressed? Overcommitted? Lost?)

- If someone is from another city/state/country and may be receiving your words through their own unique filter and not fully understanding you.

## ERADICATING GOSSIP

When we gossip, it feels crappy on all sides. So why do we do it? And better question yet, why do we love it?

According to anthropologists, gossip has been a way for us to bond with others throughout human history and is sometimes used as a tool to isolate those who aren't contributing to the greater whole. According to a study by social psychologist Laurent Bègue, about 60 percent of conversations between adults are about someone who isn't present, most often passing judgment.

There are moments when sharing frustrations about a friend or colleague with one or two confidantes can offer a perspective on how to deal with someone you care about. It can get your thoughts out of your own head and resolve the issue. When we're trying to find a solution or gain perspective on how to handle another friend's frustrating or bad behavior, I call it *Positive Gossip*.

CESSPOOL OF GOSSIP

When we feel competitive, threatened, envious, sad, hurt, or frustrated by another human or community, **Negative Gossip** is often what we turn to. Our Red Egos and Mean Girls take over. I've been the victim of Negative Gossip, as well as the aggressor when I was fearful, competitive, and wanting to feel better about myself.

In each case, it impacted my health, productivity, and happiness. Negative Gossip can lead to mistrust, which can lead to isolation, which can lead to physical and emotional unhappiness. It's the gateway to bullying.

## The ripple effect from Negative Gossip is real. It causes emotional and physical pain, sometimes for life.

When you participate in it, you join a group of people who don't feel true belonging elsewhere. People who gossip want to prove they are worthy by denigrating others. It doesn't work.

My brother-in-law Andrew has a policy in his employee manual that says, "NO GOSSIPING. We are calling you to your higher self and have zero tolerance for gossiping. If you have a problem with

## MAKE IT HAPPEN

Try a week with **NO GOSSIP** and see how it makes you feel. When your friends start talking negatively about someone, either walk away, or just say, "I'm trying not to gossip anymore. Can we talk about something else?"

someone, take a moment, think about what you want to say, and go and speak directly with them. If it's serious, document it and speak with me."

Reality check: Sometimes we can't help ourselves and want to get stuff off our chest! So if you do find yourself gossiping, here's what to do: Turn judgment into curiosity. Start with a positive statement about the person and follow it with a question that starts with "I wonder why . . ."

For example, instead of saying, "She's the worst. I can't stand working with her because she takes all the credit," try, "She's so smart and hardworking. I wonder why being a team player is hard for her?" The next step is to ask *yourself*, "I wonder why I'm so triggered by her?"

## Let's get into each other's backpacks!

If we can turn a Judgment (Mean Girl Moment) into Curiosity (Soul Sister Moment), we will undoubtedly be more empathetic and kind. It may be less juicy than dramatically telling a story, but it *physically* and *emotionally* feels better _for you_ afterward and creates an environment of kindness, trust, and possibility instead of fear and judgment. *And don't forget, the more you gossip, the more likely that you'll be a target of gossip too!* If we can't avoid it, let's at least start shifting the

CURIOSITY

GOSSIP AND JUDGMENT

*way* we gossip. And once you start putting kindness first and leave the fear behind, the energy you invested in Negative Gossip can be focused on self-development instead. You won't need to put others down in order to feel good. And ultimately, getting along is way more fun!

Conflict is unavoidable. If we can learn to look at conflict as an opportunity to grow and deepen our connection to others, we will learn to respect these moments of discomfort and stare them down courageously and with an open ear. No one wants to be the victim of gossip, and it never feels good when we put down our friends. Fear, Conflict, and Empathy are closely tied.

# Being gently aware of our triggers, fears, and sensitivities will help us move through any moments of frustration and misunderstanding into a space of belonging and connection.

Keep courageously
participating in life.
It's way more fun.

CHAPTER 9

# ℬelonging and Aging

## Live It Up as a Master Citizen

The feeling of looking at ourselves in the mirror and not recognizing the young person we *know* is still in there can be disorienting, no matter how hard we prepare for this chapter in our lives. For a host of reasons, including the media glorification of youth and what feels like the limitations of our changing bodies, we are often traumatized by the experience, begin to lose our FYF

199

attitude, and start imposing boundaries on ourselves. While there are many books on aging gracefully and aging as a spiritual practice, it's still hard! Let's just say I've been dyeing my hair since I started going gray at twenty-two.

We go from having a rich social life with school friends, work friends, and parent friends, to the kids moving away, friends moving away or dying, and often the decision to retire away from where we once lived.

We tell ourselves how hard it is to start over and rationalize our way out of socialization. Our self-imposed boundaries eventually lead to social isolation—the deadliest part of aging. Also, millions of Baby Boomers have not saved enough for retirement, and by 2030, one in four Americans will be above the age of 65. Many will hide from the shame of going from a leadership role to unemployment and food stamps and isolate themselves. As you age, it's more important than ever to find and keep your people around you!

My dear friend John, who founded Whole Foods Market and has a team of 90,000 employees and has had a loyal group of friends for more than thirty years, recently said to me: "We are ALL going to go through this process of aging— heck, it's happening to me too! The more we use this knowledge and the inevitability of death to our advantage, the less inclined we will be to take the safe and selfish route, and the more we will want to create together, deepen our relationships, share our resources, and spread love."

"Life is a grand adventure, and you can't go at it alone. Your community will give you wings to create fearlessly."

My friend Dr. Deb is a physician in her early sixties and is happily married with three amazing kids. She went from having a blond bob her entire medical career to one day deciding, in her fifties, to dye her hair hot pink and wear it in multiple braids. She also started wearing sparkly jumpsuits with platform boots. Most of her friends and family initially thought she was having a midlife crisis. But she told them she was tired and bored with living the life she was "supposed" to live. "When you're old, you're expected to cut your hair short, wear conservative clothes, go to museums and movies, play cards and golf, read about politics, and watch the news. You're expected to be a spectator of life, not a participant. If this makes you happy, great! But if you long for more and want to continue participating in this wild world and in this human form, have the courage to say the heck with what you're *supposed* to do!"

## Explore courageously at every phase!

With courage, vulnerability, and an intention to live with maniacal authenticity, Dr. Deb threw herself into the work of finding people who matched her energy and creating a community that shared her values. She found incredible new friends of all ages—

and luckily, that included me! Dr. Deb's community is now rich with interesting people and she has never been happier—and freer.

## Again, it's all about being Vulnerable, Intentional, and Courageous (VIC) at every phase of life.

I want to live in a world where intergenerational communities are the norm too. I may not want to dye my hair hot pink, but when I'm seventy, I certainly don't want to be pushed into an elderly community and spend my time only with people who are my age! I want to be able to choose the people I hang out with at every phase of life! Why can't a seventy-five-year-old go dancing and have regular, deep conversations with a thirty-year-old? And why can't a sixty-five-year-old work at a start-up? Age discrimination is real in most industries, especially in technology and at start-ups. It takes courageous leadership to hire employees of all ages to provide a wealth of perspectives in an organization.

Advertisers and marketers have segmented us into neat categories—Gen Z, Millennials, Gen X, Baby Boomers—to make it easier to sell to us (#mo'money), and as fun as it might be to be part of an "age club," it's crazy that we have created a world with invisible walls for ourselves.

And what about schools? I often wonder why we segment our kids into different grades where third graders only hang out with other third graders. Of course they're going to bully each other!

They don't have the tools or perspective to get into each other's backpacks! What if there was an intergenerational school where we brought in our elders and mixed all the kids together? It would take some educational coordination, but kids might be less likely to bully each other, and each age-group would inspire the next.

All this to say, let's recognize the power of intergenerational relationships and how they impact the perspective and balance of a community. The varying points of view I get from friends who have more life experience than me or who are younger and have a new perspective to share is invaluable. I wish I had known this earlier in my life and had been encouraged to spend more time with older and younger community members. Go through the Four Stages of Community again, this time with the view of making friends of all ages. It may just be the key to finding your people! We forget that "our people" are genderless, raceless, and ageless. It's all about energy!

Think about dating apps—they all require that you post your age to your profile page. Why does it matter? The love of our lives could be under our noses, but they may not fit the age range we put in the app! My life partner, Eli, is thirteen years younger than me, and I imagine our paths never crossing if we were both on a dating app.

The thing is, before Eli, I never would have looked twice at someone that young because of societal "norms." What a lesson it has been for me on so many levels—including recognizing that energy is ageless.

When Miki and I were twenty-three years old, we traveled to Australia for a college friend's wedding. We met twin brothers— who were *ten years old*—and they became our favorite new friends from that weekend. *Yes, they were ten years old. And we were twenty-three.* Their energy matched our energy, and we ended up playing soccer with them and laughing all weekend at the wedding! They were hilarious, and Miki and I *couldn't believe* how cool and funny they were. Our knee-jerk reactions could have been, "Hmm, is this creepy?" or "Go away, children," but we thought to ourselves, "They're just people, and they're SO MUCH FUN." We still talk about the ten-year-olds to this day.

# Energy will always be your best compass. Whenever I follow or lead with energy, it never fails me.

## Try it for your next gathering! Invite folks of all ages and see what happens!

# MAKE IT HAPPEN

In the next three months, have a really good conversation with someone who's at least ten years older than you and someone who's at least ten years younger (relatives don't count!). What do you notice about their life views? Their energy?

## MASTER CITIZENS

Here's an idea. Let's stop calling our elders "Senior Citizens" and "the Elderly." Almost 76 million Baby Boomers are 65 and over and they don't want to be called either of these derogatory terms! I looked up synonyms for *elderly* and this is some of what came up:

"No spring chicken"

"On last leg"?!

"Long in the tooth"

NO ONE IS CALLING ME ELDERLY when I turn sixty-five! Over my dead body (pun intended)!

My dad, now in his late sixties and an aerospace engineer for forty years, loves being a Boomer but was none too pleased when a grocery store clerk innocently asked him if he wanted to go through the Senior Citizens line, because it was faster. "I'm fine right where I am, thank you. I'm fitter than most forty-year-olds!" He came home grumbling and feeling bad about himself. "Do I look that old?" he asked my mom. He didn't go back to the grocery store the following week. *And this is how our self-imposed isolation begins.*

# MAKE IT HAPPEN

**What change can you inspire in your community to honor your Master Citizens more meaningfully?**

So what if instead of calling our more experienced citizens "Senior Citizens" we honored them by calling them "Master Citizens"? They say it takes 10,000 hours to become an expert at anything. At sixty-five

years old, you've clocked in 569,400 human hours. If that's not a master's degree in "humaning," then I don't know what is!

Since we all live and age differently, we can't all be described in the same way. And rather than labeling, let's reimagine how we interact with, hang out with, and honor those who have given us wings to succeed. I picture my dad getting high fives as he walks down a red-carpeted Master Citizens line at the grocery store and imagine him looking forward to going there each week with my mom. Wouldn't you want the same for the people who have helped you? And won't you want the same when you get to their age?

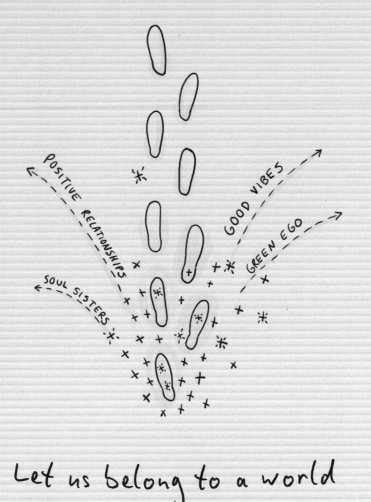

Let us belong to a world
that continues to value
soulful connections
over artificial intelligence.

# CHAPTER 10

# The Future of Belonging

## What Happens Next?

**M**y family and I spent a week in the vibrant city of San Miguel, Mexico, for the annual festival Día de los Muertos, or "Day of the Dead." For several hours we volunteered at a local community festival called La Calaca, where our friend Veronique, one of the energetic co-founders and a leader in shaping the community of San Miguel, invited us to help decorate the town square for the evening festivities. We gathered with dozens of locals in the cobblestone square, sat in a circle of wooden benches, and picked bright yellow marigolds off their green stems as we chatted in broken Spanish.

One of the volunteers played Spanish classical music on his guitar as we arranged the freshly picked flowers around a fountain in the center of the square. There was a comfort and matter-of-factness about serving the community here—a feeling of "Yeah, we're all participating, isn't that how it is everywhere?" that felt really good. This volunteer attitude and service orientation made me feel an instant sense of belonging. As I sat on the plane heading back to New York City from Mexico (with Eli, mouth open, sleeping next to me), it hit me:

# Belonging is a dance between polarities. When we dance between the "we" and the "me," magic happens.

As Americans, we have been pushed and prodded to focus on "me." We have celebrated rugged individualism, competition, independence, and "going against the grain" for so long that we've forgotten about the importance of the collective "we"—*and how good it feels*. As noted in my Hierarchy of Needs, to find joy and reach our highest human potential, we have to first find and nurture our sense of purpose and service orientation.

If our focus is only on "me," depression and anxiety *will* result. And this is what is happening. Technology has pushed us too far in the direction of isolation and individual gains (followers! likes!) that we have forgotten the dance between "me" and "we" and how important that flow is in our lives for our happiness — and survival.

# Our separation will lead to our extinction, and technological isolation is the first symptom.

This is *your* time now, and you have all the tools you need to create the best community for your life and organization.

# DO IT.

The world needs more belonging, more love, more community, and you are needed to wholeheartedly participate in receiving and sharing your energy with others. Let's reconnect to our purpose as humans—which is to simply share and receive energy. Even money is just energy! So share that generously too!

I'm concerned about the future of belonging and how humans will connect with one another in thirty to fifty years, with technology evolving at breakneck speeds and with little thought about *how* to properly use this technology. It has been well documented that there's a *direct* correlation between smartphone overuse with perceived dependence and the increase in reports of anxiety and depression.

## So why do we keep racing in the direction of more technology, especially toward virtual reality and artificial intelligence?

While I know it is our human destiny to keep evolving and pushing the boundaries of what's possible, it doesn't appear that our goals are aligned with achieving a deeper sense of belonging. If we are less happy now than we were before smartphones, why are they still our obsession? I often speak at media conferences and hear speakers bragging about how they are "increasing people's screen time with X software and Y technology." Is more screen time something to be proud of? Are we happy with how much time we're spending online, or do we later regret it? How did our sense of belonging become at the mercy of technology and capitalism? Silicon Valley is in the midst of convincing us that technology can replace the real world, that it's just a matter of triggering the right sensory experience and once we do, boom!

We've re-created reality. But this way of thinking misses one very important thing:

# ENERGY

It misses the intangible energy exchanges that happen between people and the ecosystems around us. For this reason (among others), "connecting" online is not really connecting. Even when we're simulating all five senses with virtual reality headsets and haptic gaming vests, it's a surface-level and poor excuse for real human connection. VR and artificial intelligence will never be able to touch with the warmth and energy of a human hand or hug you in a way that melts away your worries.

**Energy is the invisible universal language for all life. It's genderless, ageless, shapeless, and colorless. It's all of us. No machine could ever replicate or manufacture it.**

While technology and social media have been vital sharing tools for viral movements like #MeToo and the Women's March—even our Daybreaker community would not be where it is without it—until we fully understand the puppeteers behind the scenes playing with our attention in the name of profits (Isn't money so 2008? We've got bigger fish to fry, people!), we will continue moving farther away from true belonging.

Imagine what the world would look like if every single human felt belonging. We would show up *for real* for each other. Show up to *vote*. Show up for the *bullied kid*. Show up for the *bully*. We would embody inclusion. Focusing on the importance of belonging is essential to our existence and survival as a species. It's more apparent now than ever. Belonging might seem like an afterthought to so many of the problems we face today, but it's actually critical to solving each and every one of them.

Belonging gives us the confidence to take care of ourselves, others, our planet, and all the members of our ecosystem. Knowing this, it becomes clear that ***building a community is one of the most important, generous, and creative acts a human can aspire to***. So have the courage to follow the steps in this book at any and every turning point in your life. Keep Going IN and Going OUT. Share this with friends and support one another as you build and join new communities of your own. If you commit to participating with generous and courageous energy, you will enjoy deep belonging, abundant community, and success. Your time is now.

# LET'S GO!

If you need help architecting or creating your dream community, large or small, I'm here for you. We're launching the Belong Center, a 2.0 Community Center and Consultancy to support anyone wanting to create community anywhere in the world. If you have the courage and curiosity to nurture a community and participate in leading the revitalization of your neighborhood, local business, or global community, or create something totally new, you're the kind of person I want to support. Go to belongcenter.com for more information.

# MAKE IT HAPPEN

If you can commit to this every day for the next twenty-one days, you will reprogram your brain and will feel a deeper sense of belonging to yourself than you've felt in a long time, which will radiate into your relationships. Here it is:

Dance in front of the mirror to at least one song a day.

While you do, pay yourself compliments, love yourself, and be generous. You can be wearing clothes or be naked, alone or with a friend or partner. Remind yourself that you are just energy in human form. Remind yourself that it's incredible that you're here experiencing this wild human existence. Remind yourself that no one is judging you and that you get to choose your actions. Then just dance and let go. We spend most of our time either in our heads or being told what to do. Dance is creativity and self-expression personified. Dance is freedom. Dance is universal. It doesn't matter if you're sixteen or ninety, a man or a woman. You don't need drugs or alcohol to dance. Science has proven time and time again that dancing is the best form of exercise and the best way to release your natural D.O.S.E. No judgment. Just move. You will find after these twenty-one days that your life perspective will shift in magical ways, and you will feel a deeper sense of belonging to yourself than you've ever felt. And you will be ready to share your energy generously with others. Go to belongcenter.com for a list of songs to try!

# ACKNOWLEDGMENTS

I dedicate this book to the following humans and communities that have deeply impacted my journey:

The love of my life, my best friend and partner in mischief, Eli Clark-Davis. Your double-decker smile and giving spirit get me every time. Thank you for staying up with me every single night so I wouldn't write alone. You give me wings every day.

My OG community member—my twin sister, Miki Agrawal, who I've been in community with since we were hanging out in our mother's womb. It's unreal to have someone who knows me and who inspires me as much as you do. Thank you for being my first and oldest friend through thick and thin. From the womb to the tomb.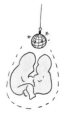

My parents, Mire and Rajendra Agrawal, who came to America as immigrants and created community from scratch with English as their second language. I watched the way you gathered our family and friends together with deep thought, intention, and play. Thank you for establishing the importance of community early in my life.

My family: my older sister, Yuri (Didi), who inspired me from the start with her adventurous spirit; to my brothers-in-law, Andrew Horn, Ben Zaitchik, and Ethan Clark-Davis, and to my parents-in-law, Rosie Clark, Jeff Davis, and Sam Horn—thank you for being such wonderful supports and sounding boards in my life; and to my nieces, Emi and Alice Zagra, and nephew, Hiro Horn-Agrawal, for reigniting my childlike wonder and for teaching me the importance of family and celebration.

My dear friends and Inner Core who brainstormed and ideated with me on so many weekends and in the middle of the night. Thank you to Max Stossel and David Yarus for your friendship, guidance, and unconditional support. And thank you to my dear friends Alfredo Rabines, Philip Donaldson, Mark Fisher, and Zach Iscol—excited to become Master Citizens together. You're home to me.

Boom Spiral Community for being tried and true FYFs and for showing up for me when I needed it most. Y'all are the crazy and wild ones and sharing this life with you has been a deep privilege.

Our Daybreaker Community and Catalysts around the world who inspired me to write this book in the first place. Thank you for saying yes and for dancing at sunrise with reckless abandon time and time again. You have been my biggest teacher and healer in every way. Our Daybreaker HQ team for being with me every step of the process as I wrote every day at our office after hours. Thank you Tim Patch, Malka Sender, Tiffany Ip, Katelyn Collins, Elliott Larue, and Aly Bloom—your gentle spirits and daily encouragement made me feel connected to the process, not just the result. You're family to me. It truly takes a village.

My soccer teams and schools: Montreal, Canada: Brossard FC Select, Harold Napper Elementary School, Centennial Regional High School, Marianopolis College; Ithaca, NY: Cornell University Varsity Soccer Team—thank you for teaching me about friendship, teamwork, and fighting together for the same goals.

My language schools: French School, Japanese School, and Hindi School—thank you for teaching me how to communicate with others across the world and for showing me the importance of diversity.

Burning Man for reminding me what radical self-expression, adventure, and inclusivity feel like. You were one of the important catalysts in my creative and community journey.

Summit Series for helping me find an Equal Energy Exchange of adventurous and curious minds.

My agents at Sterling Lord Literistic, Celeste Fine and John Maas—without your support, this book wouldn't exist. Thank you for finding the right publishing partner for this project and for making it all so easy and fun for me.

My publisher, Workman, and Susan Bolotin for believing in this book and me—it's amazing that publishers like you still exist, and it's an honor to work with you.

John Mackey for your friendship and for writing the foreword to my book. Food is the backbone and an essential building block for community, and I honor you for dedicating your life to it. Your wisdom and understanding of the human condition have been such an inspiration for me. Thank you.

To Tony Hsieh, for putting your money where your mouth is and building a community from the ground up in Vegas. You're the real deal. And to Esther Perel, Leland Melvin, Dr. Deepak Chopra, Ben Rattray, Alex Ljung, Dan Buettner, and Dr. Mark Hyman: Thank you for your endless support and for reading my book with genuine interest.

My co-illustrator, Ryan LeMere, for burning the midnight oil with me and for helping bring the pages to life. Your pictures are worth ten thousand words!

To Tomas Garcia for your cover illustration and for your incredible creative spirit.

To Lisa Hollander, Janet Vicario, James Williamson, Terri Ruffino, Jessica Rozler, Jaclyn Atkinson, and Barbara Peragine at Workman for turning my text and art into a beautifully designed and illustrated book. Thank you.

And finally, a special thank-you to my dear editor, Mary Ellen O'Neill at Workman—for being so patient and kind with me. Writing a book is such a tender experience and your keen sensibilities and edits strengthened the pages in immeasurable ways. Thank you for making this experience so wonderful and fun, and for becoming a friend in the process.

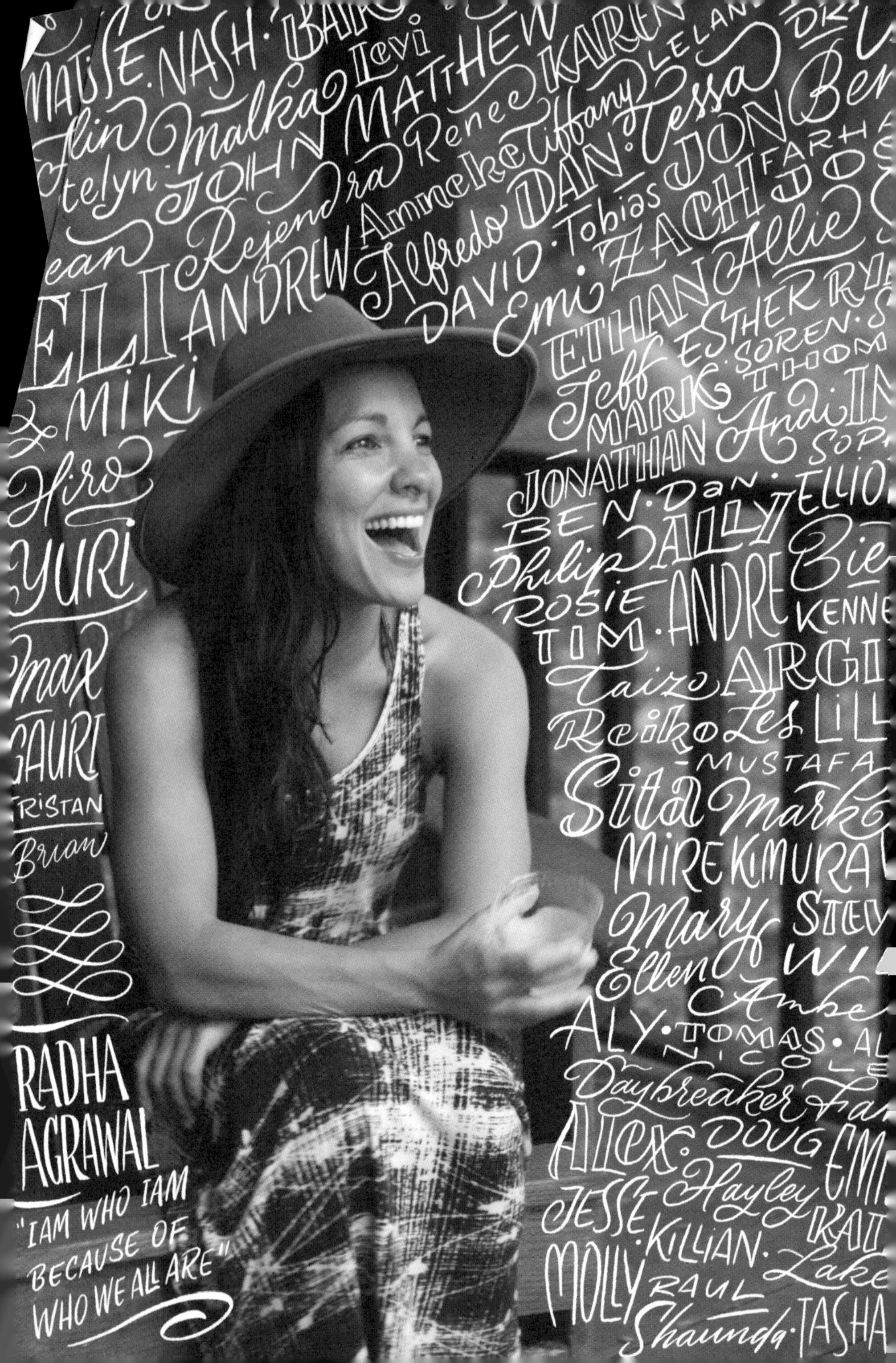

NASH
Levi
Malka
JOHN
MATTHEW
KAREN
Tiffany
Tessa
Rene
Rejendra
Anneke
Alfredo
DAN
JON
ANDREW
ELI
MIKI
Hiro
YURI
max
GAURI
Brian
DAVID
Tobias
ZACH
Emi
ETHAN
Allie
ESTHER
Jeff
SOREN
MARK
NATHAN
Andi
JONATHAN
BEN
Dan
SALLY
Philip
ROSIE
TIM
ANDRE
Taizo
Reiko
Les
MUSTAFA
Sita
Mark
MIRE KIMURA
Mary
Ellen
ALY
TOMAS
NICOLE
Daybreaker
ALEX
DOUG
JESSE
Hayley
KILLIAN
MOLLY
RAUL
Lake
Shaunda
TASHA
RADHA AGRAWAL
"I AM WHO I AM BECAUSE OF WHO WE ALL ARE"

# ABOUT THE AUTHOR

Radha Agrawal loves people. She is the Co-founder, CEO, and Chief Community Architect of Daybreaker, the early morning dance and wellness move-ment that currently holds events in twenty-five cities and on a dozen college campuses around the world and has an active community of almost half a million people. A highly recognized entrepreneur (Co-founder of THINX and LiveItUp), speaker, inventor, and investor, Radha most recently launched The Belong Center, a comprehensive Community Architecture and Experience Design Lab for individuals, progressive organizations, universities, and brands interested in creating meaningful communities. She was named by MTV as "one of 8 women who will change the world." Radha lives in Brooklyn, New York, with her love, Eli, and her twin sister, Miki—and lots of family and friends within a few blocks. You can most often find her tinkering with community and experience design projects or on the dance floor at Daybreaker in New York City (if she's not dancing at sunrise in another part of the world).

Photograph by HORTENSE MULLIEZ